DURANG/ DURANG

BY
CHRISTOPHER DURANG

★

★

DRAMATISTS
PLAY SERVICE
INC.

Table of Contents

AUTHOR'S NOTE

DURANG/DURANG was the first full theatrical evening I had presented in New York City since LAUGHING WILD in 1987.

I like to help guide actors and directors to find the best tone for presenting my plays; and so at the end of the play scripts, I include some rather substantial author's notes for the production of these six one act plays.

I offer these notes as suggestions and as help.

Christoper Durang
December 1995
New York City

MRS. SORKEN

MRS. SORKEN was the opening play of the six-play evening, DURANG/DURANG, produced by Manhattan Theatre Club (Lynne Meadow, Artistic Director; Barry Grove, Managing Director) in New York City on November 14, 1994. It was directed by Walter Bobbie; the set design was by Derek McLane; the costume design was by David C. Woolard; the lighting design was by Brian Nason; the sound design was by Tony Meola; the production stage manager was Perry Cline and the stage manager was Gregg Fletcher. The cast was as follows:

MRS. SORKEN .... Patricia Elliott

A previous version of MRS. SORKEN was presented by American Repertory Theatre in Cambridge, Massachusetts, with Elizabeth Franz playing Mrs. Sorken. Also, E. Katherine Kerr played another version of Mrs. Sorken at the Westport Artists Theatre Workshop in Westport, Connecticut.

In DURANG/DURANG there was one intermission, after the third play. The program included this listing:

ACT ONE: Theatre
ACT TWO: Everything Else.

The 6 plays had a company of seven actors: Becky Ann Baker, David Aaron Baker, Patricia Elliott, Marcus Giamatti, Lizbeth Mackay, Patricia Randell, Keith Reddin. Understudies were John Augustine, Judith Hawking, Margo Skinner.

MRS. SORKEN

Enter Mrs. Sorken to address the audience. She is a charming woman, well-dressed and gracious, though a little scattered. She is happy to be there.

MRS. SORKEN. Dear theatergoers, welcome, and how lovely to see you. I've come here to talk to you about theatre, and why we all leave our homes to come see it, assuming we have. But you have left your homes, and you're here. So, welcome!

Now I have written down some comments about theatre for you, if I can just find them. *(Searches through her purse.)*

Isn't it refreshing to see someone with a purse? *(Looks some more through the purse.)*

Well, I can't find my notes, so I'll have to make my comments from memory.

Drama. Let's begin with etymology, shall we?... etymology, which is the history of the word.

The word "drama" comes from the Greek word "dran," which means to do, and which connects with the English word "drain," meaning to exhaust one totally, and with the modern pharmaceutical sedating tablet, Dramamine, which is the trade name of a drug used to relieve airsickness and seasickness and a general sense of nausea, or "nausée" as Jean Paul Sartre might say, perhaps over a cup of espresso at a Paris bistro. How I love Paris in the spring, or would, if I had ever been there; but Mr. Sorken and I haven't done much traveling. Maybe after he dies I'll go somewhere.

We go to the drama seeking the metaphorical Dramamine that will cure us of our nausea of life.

Of course, sometimes we become nauseated by the drama itself, and then we are sorry we went, especially if it uses the

F-word and lasts over four hours. I don't mind a leisurely play, but by 10:30 I want to leave the theatre and go to sleep. Frequently, I prefer Dramamine to drama, and only wish someone would renew my prescription for Seconal.

Secondly ... we have the word "theatre," which is derived from the Greek word "theasthai," which means to view.

And nowadays we have the word, "reastat," a device by which we can dim the lights in one's house slowly, rather than just snapping them off with a simple switch.

And thirdly, we have the Greek god "Dionysus," the last syllable of which is spelled "s-u-s" in English, but "s-o-s" in Greek, the letters which in Morse code spell *help* — "Dionysos" is the god of wine and revelry, but also the father of modern drama as we know it.

The Greeks went to the theatre in the open air, just like the late and wonderful Joseph Papp used to make us see Shakespeare. Shakespeare's language is terribly difficult to understand for us of the modern age, but how much easier it is when there's a cool breeze and it's for free. If it's hot and I have to pay, well, then I don't much like Shakespeare. I'm sorry, I shouldn't say that. He's a brilliant writer, and I look forward to seeing all 750 of his plays. Although perhaps not in this lifetime.

But back to the Greeks. They went to the open-air theatre expecting the drama they saw to evoke terror and pity.

Nowadays we have enough terror and pity in our own lives, and so rather than going to the theatre looking for terror, we go looking for slight irritation. And rather than looking for the theatre to evoke pity, we look merely for a generalized sense of identification as in "Evita was a woman, I am a woman." Or "Sweeney Todd was a barber, I go to the hairdresser." Or "Fosca in *Passion* should have her moles removed, I know a good dermatologist." That sort of thing.

But did the Greeks really experience terror and pity? And if so, what was it in all that matricide-patricide that so affected them?

I know that seeing Greek drama nowadays, even with Diana Rigg in it, really rather baffles me, it is so very different from my own life. My life with Mr. Sorken is not something that Diana Rigg would wish to star in, even on PBS. My life is not all that interesting.

Indeed, addressing you at this very moment, I'm sorry to say, is the high point of my life to date.

Could I have lived my life differently? Women of my generation were encouraged to marry and to play the piano, and I have done both those things. Is there a piano here? I don't see one. I might have played a sonata for you, or a polonaise.

But back to my theme — Drama, from the Greek word "dran."

When we leave the drama, we return to our homes feeling "drained." And if it's been a good night in the theatre, we leave feeling slightly irritated; and feeling identification with Evita or Fosca or that poor Mormon woman in *Angels in America*.

And so, drained, we get into our nightgowns, we adjust our reastats from light to darkness, we climb into bed next to Mr. Sorken, we fall into a deep REM sleep, dreaming God-knows-what mysterious messages from our teeming unconscious; and then in the morning we open our eyes to the light of the new day, of the burgeoning possibilities.

Light from the Greek word "leukos," meaning white, and the Latin word "lumen" meaning illumination. In German, *der licht;* in French, *la lumière*. All art leads to light.

Light. Plants need light to grow. Might people need art to grow? It's possible. Are people less important than plants? Some of them are certainly less interesting.

But there is some connection between theatre and light, and people and plants, that I am striving to articulate. It's about photosynthesis, I think, which is the ingestion of light that plants go through in order to achieve growth.

And you see, it's "light" again — "photo" comes from the Greek word, "phos," which means light and which relates to phosphorescence, or the "light given off." And "synthesis" comes from the Greek prefix, "syn–" meaning together, and the Greek word "tithenai," meaning to place, to put.

Photosynthesis — to put it together with light.

We go to the theatre, desperate for help in photosynthesis.

The text of the play is the light, the actors help put it together, and we are the plants in the audience.

Plants, lights, theatre, art. I feel this sense of sudden interconnection with everything that's making me feel dizzy. And Dramamine, of course, is good for dizziness.

Now, to wrap up.

(Warmly.) Welcome, theatergoers. I hope you enjoy this evening. Act One is theatre parodies. Act Two ... is not.

The plays are by Christopher Durang, who is one of my favorite writers. He is also my nephew. If David Mamet was my nephew, I'm sure he'd be my favorite writer as well. Although, in truth, I don't think Mr. Mamet would have an aunt like me. I think if he has any aunts, they are probably Chicago gangsters who use the F-word. I'm sorry, was that rude? But anyway, please enjoy this evening. And if you are ever in Connecticut, I hope you'll drop in and say hello to me and Mr. Sorken. He prefers that you call first, but I love to be surprised. So just ring the bell, and we'll have cocktails.

And I hope you have enjoyed my humbly offered comments on the drama. I have definitely enjoyed speaking with you, and have a sneaking suspicion that in the future, it is going to be harder and harder to shut me up. (Rather grandly raises her arms upward to present the evening that is to follow.)

Let the games begin! (Lights out.)

FOR WHOM THE SOUTHERN BELLE TOLLS

SOUTHERN BELLE TOLLS

(or "The Further Adventures of
Amanda and Her Children")

FOR WHOM THE SOUTHERN BELLE TOLLS was part of the six-play evening, DURANG/DURANG, produced at Manhattan Theatre Club (Lynne Meadow, Artistic Director; Barry Grove, Managing Director) in New York City on November 14, 1994. It was directed by Walter Bobbie; the set design was by Derek McLane; the costume design was by David C. Woolard; the lighting design was by Brian Nason; the sound design was by Tony Meola; the production stage manager was Perry Cline and the stage manager was Gregg Fletcher. The cast was as follows:

AMANDA .... Lizbeth Mackay
LAWRENCE .... Keith Reddin
TOM .... David Aaron Baker
GINNY .... Patricia Randell

The spring before this production, the play was presented by Ensemble Studio Theatre in New York City (Curt Dempster, Artistic Director; Kevin Confoy, Managing Director) as part of its one-act Marathon '94. The cast and the director were the same.

Several years before these two productions, there was a showcase production of an earlier version of BELLE. It was directed by Scott Allen, and its cast was Laura Waterbury as Amanda, John Money as Lawrence, Timothy Kivel as Tom, and Julie Knight as Ginny.

And subsequent to that showcase, there were two staged readings of BELLE, one at the Westport Artists Theatre Workshop in Connecticut, and one at a benefit for The Glines Theatre in New York City. Both times E. Katherine Kerr and Christopher Durang played Amanda and Lawrence; and John Augustine and Julie Janney were Tom and Ginny in Westport, and Jeffrey Hayenga and Cristine Rose were Tom and Ginny at the Glines benefit.

FOR WHOM THE SOUTHERN BELLE TOLLS

(or "The Further Adventures
of Amanda and Her Children")

*A warm, fussy living room setting. A couch, a chair, homey
and warm. Maybe a fringed throw over the couch. Maybe a
vase of jonquils.*

*Enter Amanda, the Southern belle mother. Dressed nicely, for
company. Feminine clothing, though perhaps a feeling of an
earlier time to what she's wearing.*

AMANDA.   Rise and shine! Rise and shine! *(Calls off.)*
Lawrence, honey, come on out here and let me have a look
at you! *(Enter Lawrence, who limps across the room. In his 20s, or
maybe a young-looking 30, he is very sensitive, and is wearing what
are clearly his dress clothes. Amanda fiddles with his bow tie and
stands back to admire him.)* Lawrence, honey, you look lovely.
LAWRENCE.   No, I don't, mama. I have a pimple on the
back of my neck.
AMANDA.   Don't say the word "pimple," honey, it's common.
(With hopeful energy.) Now your brother Tom is bringing home
a girl from the warehouse for you to meet, and I want you to
make a good impression, honey.
LAWRENCE.   It upsets my stomach to meet people, mama.
AMANDA.   Oh, Lawrence honey, you're so sensitive it makes
me want to hit you.
LAWRENCE.   I don't need to meet people, mama. I'm happy
just by myself, playing with my collection of glass cocktail stirrers. *(Lawrence smiles wanly and limps over to a table on top of
which sits a glass jar filled with glass swizzle sticks.)*

AMANDA.   Lawrence, you are a caution. Only retarded people and alcoholics are interested in glass cocktail stirrers.

LAWRENCE.   *(With proud wonderment.)* Each one of them has a special name, mama. *(Picks up one to show her.)* This one is called Stringbean because it's long and thin. *(Picks up another one.)* And this one is called Stringbean because it's long and thin. *(Picks up a blue one.)* And this one is called blue because it's blue.

AMANDA.   All my children have such imagination, why was I so blessed? Oh, Lawrence honey, how are you going to get on in the world if you just stay home all day, year after year, playing with your collection of glass cocktail stirrers?

LAWRENCE.   I don't like the world, mama. I like it here in this room.

AMANDA.   I know you do, Lawrence honey, that's part of your charm. Some days. But, *honey*, what about making a living?

LAWRENCE.   I can't work, mama. I'm crippled. *(He limps over to the couch and sits.)*

AMANDA.   *(Firmly.)* There is nothing wrong with your leg, Lawrence honey, all the doctors have told you that. This limping thing is an *affectation.*

LAWRENCE.   *(Perhaps a little steely.)* I only know how I feel, mama.

AMANDA.   Oh if only I had connections in the Mafia, I'd have someone come and break *both* your legs.

LAWRENCE.   *(Slightly amused.)* Don't try to make me laugh, mama. You know I have asthma.

AMANDA.   Your asthma, your leg, your eczema. You're just a mess, Lawrence!

LAWRENCE.   I have scabs from the itching, mama.

AMANDA.   That's lovely, Lawrence. You must tell us more over dinner.

LAWRENCE.   Alright.

AMANDA.   That was a *joke*, Lawrence.

LAWRENCE.   Don't try to make me laugh, mama. My asthma.

AMANDA.   Now, Lawrence, I don't want you talking about your ailments to the feminine caller your brother Tom is bringing home from the warehouse, honey. No nice-bred young lady likes to hear a young man discussing his eczema, Lawrence.

LAWRENCE. What else can I talk about, mama?

AMANDA. Talk about the weather. Or Red China.

LAWRENCE. Or my collection of glass cocktail stirrers?

AMANDA. I suppose so, honey, if the conversation's come to some God-awful standstill. Otherwise, I'd shut up about it. *(Becomes coquettish, happy memories.)* Conversation is an art, Lawrence. Back at Blue Mountain, when I had seventeen gentlemen callers, I was able to converse with charm and vivacity for six hours without stop and never once mention eczema or bone cancer or vivisection. Try to emulate me, Lawrence honey. Charm and vivacity. And charm. And vivacity. And charm.

LAWRENCE. Well, I'll try, but I doubt it.

AMANDA. Me too, honey. But we'll go through the motions anyway, won't we?

LAWRENCE. I don't know if I want to meet some girl who works in a warehouse, mama.

AMANDA. Your brother Tom says she's a lovely girl with a nice personality. And where else does he meet girls except the few who work at the warehouse? He only seems to meet men at the movies. *(Thinking it's odd, but not sure why.)* Your brother goes to the movies entirely too much. I must speak to him about it.

LAWRENCE. It's unfeminine for a girl to work at a warehouse.

AMANDA. *(Firm, frustrated.)* Now Lawrence — if you can't go out the door without getting an upset stomach or an attack of vertigo, then we have got to find some nice girl who's willing to *support* you. Otherwise, how am I ever going to get you out of this house and off my hands?

LAWRENCE. *(Sensitive, unknowing.)* Why do you want to be rid of me, mama?

AMANDA. I suppose it's unmotherly of me, dear, but you really get on my nerves. Limping around the apartment, pretending to have asthma. If only some nice girl would marry you and I knew you were taken care of, then I'd feel free to start to live again. I'd join Parents without Partners, I'd go to dinner dances, I'd have a life again. Rather than just watch you mope about this stupid apartment. I'm not bitter, dear, it's just that I hate my life.

LAWRENCE. I understand, mama.

AMANDA. Do you, dear? Oh, you're cute. Oh, listen, I think I hear them.

TOM. *(From offstage.)* Mother, I forgot my key.

LAWRENCE. I'll be in the other room. *(Starts to limp away.)*

AMANDA. I want you to let them in, Lawrence.

LAWRENCE. Oh, I couldn't, mama. She'd see I limp.

AMANDA. Then don't limp, damn it.

TOM. *(From off.)* Mother, are you there?

AMANDA. Just a minute, Tom, honey. Now, Lawrence, you march over to that door or I'm going to break all your swizzle sticks.

LAWRENCE. Mama, I can't!

AMANDA. Lawrence, you are a grown boy. Now you answer that door like any normal person.

LAWRENCE. I can't.

TOM. *(From off.)* Mother, I'm going to break the door down in a minute.

AMANDA. Just be patient, Tom. Now you're causing a scene, Lawrence. I want you to answer that door.

LAWRENCE. My eczema itches.

AMANDA. *(Impatient.)* I'll itch it for you in a second, Lawrence.

TOM. *(From off.)* Alright, I'm breaking it down. *(Sound of door breaking down. Enter Tom and Ginny Bennett, a vivacious, friendly girl dressed in either factory clothes, or else a simple, not too-frilly blouse and slacks.)*

AMANDA. Oh, Tom, you got in.

TOM. *(Very angry.)* Why must we go through this every night??? You know the stupid fuck won't open the door, so why don't you let him alone about it? *(To Ginny.)* My kid brother has a thing about answering doors. He thinks people will notice his limp and his asthma and his eczema.

16

LAWRENCE. Excuse me. I think I hear someone calling me in the other room. (*Limps off, calls to imaginary person.*) Coming! (*Exits.*)

AMANDA. (*Angry, focused on Tom.*) Now see what you've done. He's probably going to refuse to come to the table due to your insensitivity. Oh, was any woman as cursed as I? With one son who's too sensitive and another one who's this big lox. (*Suddenly re-notices Ginny; switches to Southern charm and graciousness.*) I'm sorry, how rude of me. I'm Amanda Wingvalley. You must be Virginia Bennett from the warehouse. Tom has spoken so much about you I feel you're almost one of the family, preferably a daughter-in-law. Welcome, Virginia.

GINNY. (*Very friendly, and very loud.*) CALL ME GINNY OR GIN! BUT JUST DON'T CALL ME "LATE FOR DINNER"!!! (*Roars with laughter.*)

AMANDA. Oh, how amusing. (*Whispers to Tom.*) Why is she shouting? Is she deaf?

GINNY. (*Still talking loudly.*) You're asking why I am speaking loudly. It's so that I can be heard! I am taking a course in public speaking, and so far we've covered organizing your thoughts and speaking good and loud so the people in the back of the room can hear you.

AMANDA. Public speaking. How impressive. You must be interested in improving yourself.

GINNY. (*Truly not having heard.*) What?

AMANDA. (*Loudly.*) YOU MUST BE INTERESTED IN IMPROVING YOURSELF.

GINNY. (*Loudly and happily.*) YES I AM!

TOM. When's dinner? I want to get this over with fast if everyone's going to shout all evening.

GINNY. What?

AMANDA. (*To Ginny.*) Dinner is almost ready.

GINNY. Who's Freddy?

AMANDA. Oh, Lord. No, dear. DINNER IS READY.

GINNY. Oh good. I'm as hungry as a bear! (*Growls enthusiastically.*)

AMANDA. You must be very *popular* at the warehouse, Ginny.

GINNY. No popsicle for me, ma'am, although I will take

you up on some gin.

AMANDA. *(Confused.)* What?

GINNY. *(Loudly.)* I WOULD LIKE SOME GIN.

AMANDA. Well, fine. I think I'd like to get drunk too. Tom, why don't you go and make two Southern ladies some nice summer gin and tonics? And see if sister would like a lemonade.

TOM. Sister?

AMANDA. I'm sorry, did I say sister? I meant brother.

TOM. *(Calling as he exits.)* Hey, four eyes, you wanna lemonade?

AMANDA. Tom's so amusing. He calls Lawrence "four eyes" even though he doesn't wear glasses.

GINNY. And does *Lawrence* wear glasses?

AMANDA. *(Confused.)* What?

GINNY. You said Tom called Lawrence "four eyes" even though he doesn't wear glasses, and I wondered if *Lawrence* wore glasses. Because that would, you see, explain it.

AMANDA. *(Looks at her with despair.)* Ah. I don't know. I'll have to ask Lawrence someday. *(Switches to energy, and Southern charm again.)* Speaking of Lawrence, let me go check on the supper and see if I can convince him to come out here and make conversation with you.

GINNY. No, thank you, ma'am, I'll just have the gin.

AMANDA. What?

GINNY. What?

AMANDA. Never mind. I'll be back. Or with luck I won't. *(Amanda exits. Ginny looks around uncomfortably, and sees the table with the collection of glass cocktail stirrers.)*

GINNY. *(Looking at stirrers.)* They must drink a lot here. *(Enter Tom with a glass for Ginny.)*

TOM. Here's some gin for Ginny. *(Offers drink.)*

GINNY. What? *(Doesn't take drink.)*

TOM. Here's your poison.

GINNY. No, thanks, I'll just wait here. *(Ginny now notices the offered drink, and takes it.)*

TOM. Have you ever thought that your hearing is being affected by all that loud *machinery* at the warehouse?

GINNY. Scenery? You mean, like trees? Yeah, I like trees.

TOM. I like trees too. *(Tom sort of gives up on conversation, and leafs through his newspaper.)*

AMANDA. *(From offstage.)* Now you get out of that bed this minute, Lawrence Wingvalley, or I'm going to give that over-bearing girl your *entire* collection of glass gobbledygook — is that clear? *(Amanda pushes in Lawrence, who is wearing a blue night shirt.)* I believe Lawrence would like to visit with you, Ginny.

GINNY. *(Shows her drink.)* Tom brought me my drink already, thank you, Mrs. Wingvalley.

AMANDA. You know, dear, a *hearing aid* isn't really all that expensive, you might look into that.

GINNY. No, if I have the gin, I don't really want any Gatorade. Never liked the stuff anyway. But you feel free.

AMANDA. Thank you, dear. I will. *(Takes Tom by the arm, to lead him away; back to charm.)* Come, Tom, come to the kitchen and help me prepare the supper. And we'll let the two young people converse. Remember, Lawrence. Charm and vivacity.

TOM. *(Putting down his newspaper.)* I hope this dinner won't take long, mother. I don't want to get to the movies too late.

AMANDA. *(Irritated.)* Oh shut up about the movies. *(Smiles charmingly at Ginny and Lawrence. Amanda and Tom exit. Lawrence stands still, uncomfortably. Ginny looks at him pleasantly. Brief pause.)*

GINNY. *(Loudly.)* HI.

LAWRENCE. *(Startled.)* Hi ... I'd gone to bed.

GINNY. I never eat bread. It's too fattening. I have to watch my figure if I want to get ahead in the world. *(Suddenly wondering.)* Why are you wearing that nightshirt?

LAWRENCE. I'd gone to bed. I wasn't feeling well. My leg hurts, and I have a headache, and I have palpitations of the heart.

GINNY. I don't know. Hum a few bars, and I'll see.

LAWRENCE. *(Hears her odd statement, can't figure it out; says shyly:)* We've met before, you know.

GINNY. Uh huh.

LAWRENCE. *(Telling a precious memory.)* We were in high

school together. You were voted Girl Most Likely to Succeed. We sat next to one another in glee club.

GINNY.   I'm sorry, I really can't hear you. You're talking too softly.

LAWRENCE.   *(Louder.)* You used to call me BLUE ROSES.

GINNY.   BLUE ROSES? Oh yes, I remember, sort of. Why did I do that?

LAWRENCE.   I had been absent from school for several months, and when I came back, you asked me where I'd been, and I said I'd been sick with viral pneumonia, but you thought I said "blue roses."

GINNY.   I didn't get much of that, but I remember you now. You used to make a spectacle of yourself every day in glee class, clumping up the aisle with this great big noisy leg brace on your leg. God, you made a racket!

LAWRENCE.   *(Sensitive, embarrassed.)* I was always so afraid people were looking at me, and pointing. *(A bit resentful.)* But then eventually mama wouldn't let me wear the leg brace anymore. She gave it to the salvation army.

GINNY.   I've never been in the army. How long were you in for?

LAWRENCE.   I've never been in the army. I have asthma.

GINNY.   You do? May I see it?

LAWRENCE.   *(Confused.)* See it?

GINNY.   Well, sure, unless you don't want to.

LAWRENCE.   Maybe you want to see my collection of glass cocktail stirrers. *(Lawrence limps to the table where his precious collection is. Ginny follows behind him. Holds up a swizzle stick.)* I call this one Stringbean, because it's long and thin.

GINNY.   Thank you. *(Cheerfully puts it in her glass and stirs it.)*

LAWRENCE.   *(Fairly appalled.)* They're not for *use. (Takes it back from her.)* They're a collection.

GINNY.   *(Not having heard, but willing.)* Well I guess I stirred it enough.

LAWRENCE.   They're my favorite thing in the world. *(Holds up another one.)* I call this one Q-tip, because I realized it looks like a Q-tip, except it's made out of glass and doesn't have little cotton swabs at the end of it. *(Ginny looks blank.)* Q-TIP.

GINNY. Really? *(Takes it and puts it in her ear.)*
LAWRENCE. No!!! Don't put it in your ear. *(Takes it back.)*
Now it's disgusting.
GINNY. Well, I didn't think it was a Q-tip, but that's what
you said it was.
LAWRENCE. I *call* it that. I think I'm going to throw it out
now. *(Puts Q-Tip aside somewhere; holds up another one.)* I call this
one Pinocchio because if you hold it perpendicular to your
nose it makes your nose look long. *(Holds it up to his nose.)*
GINNY. Uh huh.
LAWRENCE. *(Holds up another one.)* And I call this one Henry
Kissinger, because he wears glasses and it's made of glass.
GINNY. Uh huh. *(Takes it and stirs her drink again.)*
LAWRENCE. No! They're just for looking, not for stirring.
(Calls.) Mama, she's making a mess with my collection.
AMANDA. *(From off.)* Oh shut up about your collection,
honey, you're probably driving the poor girl bananas.
GINNY. *(Calls off to her.)* No bananas, thank you! My nutri-
tionist says I should avoid potassium. *(To Lawrence.)* You know
what I take your trouble to be, Lawrence?
LAWRENCE. Mama says I'm retarded.
GINNY. I know you're tired, I figured that's why you put
on the nightshirt, but this won't take long. I judge you to be
lacking in self-confidence. Am I right?
LAWRENCE. Well, I am afraid of people and things, and I
have a lot of ailments.
GINNY. But that makes you special, Lawrence.
LAWRENCE. What does?
GINNY. I don't know. Whatever you said. And that's why
you should present yourself with more confidence. Throw back
your shoulders, and say, "HI! HOW YA DOIN'?" Now you try
it.
LAWRENCE. *(Unenthusiastically, softly.)* Hello. How are you?
GINNY. *(Looking at watch, in response to his supposed question.)*
I don't know, it's about 8:30, but this won't take long and then
you can go to bed. Alright, now try it. *(Booming.)* "HI! HOW
YA DOIN'?"
LAWRENCE. Hi. How ya doin'?

21

GINNY.   Now swagger a bit. *(Kinda butch.)* HI. HOW YA DOIN'?

LAWRENCE.   *(Imitates her fairly successfully.)* HI. HOW YA DOIN'?

GINNY.   Good, Lawrence. That's much better. Again. *(Lawrence starts to enjoy this game with Ginny. Amanda and Tom enter from behind them and watch this.)* HI! HOW YA DOIN'?

LAWRENCE.   HI! HOW YA DOIN'?

GINNY.   THE BRAVES PLAYED A HELLUVA GAME, DON'TCHA THINK?

LAWRENCE.   THE BRAVES PLAYED A HELLUVA GAME, DON'TCHA THINK?

AMANDA.   Oh God I feel sorry for their children. Is this the *only* girl who works at the warehouse, Tom?

GINNY.   HI, MRS. WINGVALLEY. YOUR SON LAWRENCE AND I ARE GETTING ON JUST FINE, AREN'T WE, LAWRENCE?

AMANDA.   Please, no need to shout, I'm not deaf, even if you are.

GINNY.   What?

AMANDA.   I'm glad you like Lawrence.

GINNY.   What?

AMANDA.   I'M GLAD YOU LIKE LAWRENCE.

GINNY.   What?

AMANDA.   WHY DON'T YOU MARRY LAWRENCE?

GINNY.   *(Looks shocked; has heard this.)* Oh.

LAWRENCE.   Oh, mama.

GINNY.   Oh dear, I see. So that's why Shakespeare asked me here.

AMANDA.   *(To Tom.)* Shakespeare?

TOM.   The first day of work she asked me my name, and I said Tom Wingvalley, and she thought I said Shakespeare.

GINNY.   Oh dear. Mrs. Wingvalley, if I had a young brother as nice and as special as Lawrence is, I'd invite girls from the warehouse home to meet him too.

AMANDA.   *(Retreating to vague manners.)* I'm sure I don't know what you mean.

GINNY.   And you're probably hoping I'll say that I'll call

again.

AMANDA.   Really, we haven't even had supper yet. Tom, shouldn't you be checkin' on the roast pigs feet?

TOM.   I guess so. If anything interesting happens, call me. *(Exits.)*

GINNY.   But I'm afraid I won't be calling on Lawrence again.

LAWRENCE.   This is so embarrassing. I told you I wanted to stay in my room.

AMANDA.   Hush up, Lawrence.

GINNY.   But, Lawrence, I don't want you to think that I won't be calling because I don't like you. I do like you. *(Lawrence and Amanda both look hopeful.)*

LAWRENCE.   You do?

GINNY.   Sure. I like everybody. But I got two time clocks to punch, Mrs. Wingvalley. One at the warehouse, and one at night.

AMANDA.   At night? You have a second job? That *is* ambitious.

GINNY.   Not a second job, ma'am. Betty.

AMANDA.   Pardon?

GINNY.   Now who's deaf, eh what? Betty. I'm involved with a girl named Betty. We've been going together for about a year. We're saving money so that we can buy a farmhouse and a tractor together. So you can see why I can't visit your son, though I wish I could. *(To Lawrence.)* No hard feelings, Lawrence. You're a good kid. *(Lawrence looks extremely crushed and sad. He limps over to his collection, and takes one of his precious swizzle sticks, and offers it to Ginny.)*

LAWRENCE.   I want you to keep this. It's my very favorite one. I call it thermometer because it looks like a thermometer.

GINNY.   You want me to have this?

LAWRENCE.   Yes, as a souvenir.

GINNY.   *(Offended.)* Well, there's no need to call me a queer. Fuck you and your stupid swizzle sticks. *(Throws the offered gift upstage.)*

LAWRENCE.   *(Horrified.)* You've broken it!

GINNY.   What?

LAWRENCE.   You've broken it. YOU'VE BROKEN IT.

GINNY.   So I've broken it. Big fuckin' deal. You have twenty more of them here.

AMANDA.   Well, I'm so sorry you have to be going.

GINNY.   What?

AMANDA.   Hadn't you better be going?

GINNY.   What?

AMANDA.   GO AWAY!

GINNY.   *(Hearing the last phrase.)* Well I guess I can tell when I'm not wanted. I guess I'll go now.

AMANDA.   You and Betty must come over some evening. Preferably when we're out.

GINNY.   Uh huh. *(Calls off.)* So long, Shakespeare. See you at the warehouse. *(To Lawrence.)* So long, Lawrence. I hope your rash gets better.

LAWRENCE.   *(Saddened, holding the broken swizzle stick.)* You broke thermometer.

GINNY.   What?

LAWRENCE.   YOU BROKE THERMOMETER!

GINNY.   WELL, WHAT WAS A THERMOMETER DOING IN WITH THE SWIZZLE STICKS ANYWAY?

LAWRENCE.   ITS *NAME* WAS THERMOMETER, YOU NIT-WIT!

AMANDA.   Let it go, Lawrence. There'll be other swizzle sticks. Goodbye, Virginia.

GINNY.   I sure am hungry. Any chance I might be able to take a sandwich with me?

AMANDA.   Certainly you can shake hands with me, if that will make you happy.

GINNY.   I said I'm *hungry.*

AMANDA.   Really, dear? What part of Hungary are you from?

GINNY.   Oh never mind. I guess I'll go.

AMANDA.   That's right. You have two time clocks. It must be getting near to when you punch in Betty.

GINNY.   *(Cheerful, her basic nature.)* Well, so long, everybody! I had a nice time. *(Exits. Quiet. Amanda walks toward the kitchen and calls off to Tom in a contained voice.)*

AMANDA.   Tom, come in here please. Lawrence, I don't believe I would play the Victrola right now.

LAWRENCE. What Victrola?

AMANDA. Any Victrola. *(Enter Tom.)*

TOM. Yes, mother? Where's Ginny?

AMANDA. The feminine caller made a hasty departure.

TOM. Old four eyes bored her to death, huh?

LAWRENCE. Oh, drop dead.

TOM. We should have you institutionalized.

AMANDA. That's the first helpful thing you've said all evening, but first things first. You played a little joke on us, Tom.

TOM. What are you talking about?

AMANDA. You didn't mention that your friend is already spoken for.

TOM. Really? I didn't even think she *liked* men.

AMANDA. Yes, well. It seems odd that you know so little about a person you see everyday at the warehouse.

TOM. The warehouse is where I work, not where I know things about people.

AMANDA. The disgrace. The expense of the pigs feet, a new tie for Lawrence. And you — bringing a lesbian into this house. Why, we haven't had a lesbian in this house since your grandmother died. And now you have the audacity to bring in that ... that ...

LAWRENCE. Dyke.

AMANDA. Thank you, Lawrence. That overbearing, booming-voiced bull dyke. Into a Christian home.

TOM. Oh look, who cares? No one in their right mind would marry four eyes here.

AMANDA. You have no Christian charity, or filial devotion, or fraternal affection.

TOM. I don't want to listen to this. I'm going to the movies.

AMANDA. You go to the movies to excess, Tom. It isn't healthy.

LAWRENCE. While you're out, could you stop at the liquor store and get me some more cocktail stirrers? She broke thermometer, and she put Q-tip in her ear.

AMANDA. Listen to your brother, Tom. He's pathetic. How are we going to support ourselves once you go? And I know you want to leave. I've seen the brochure for the merchant marines in your underwear drawer. And the application to the air force. And your letter of inquiry to the Ballet Trockadero. So I'm not unaware of what you're thinking. But don't leave us until you fulfill your duties here, Tom. Help brother find a wife, or a job, or a doctor. Or consider euthanasia. But don't leave me here all alone, saddled with him.

LAWRENCE.   Mama, don't you like me?

AMANDA.   Of course, dear. I'm just making jokes.

LAWRENCE.   Be careful of my asthma.

AMANDA.   I'll try, dear. Now why don't you hold your breath in case you get a case of terminal hiccups?

LAWRENCE.   *(Willing; a new possible ailment.)* Alright. *(Holds his breath.)*

TOM.   *(Fed up with everything.)* I'm leaving.

AMANDA.   Where are you going?

TOM.   I'm going to the movies.

AMANDA.   I don't believe you go to the movies. What did you see last night?

TOM.   *(Somewhat defiant.)* Hyapatia Lee in *Beaver City.*

AMANDA.   And the night before that?

TOM.   I don't remember. *Humpy Bus Boys* or something.

AMANDA.   Humpy what?

TOM.   Nothing! Leave me alone!

AMANDA.   These are not mainstream movies, Tom. Why can't you see a normal movie like *The Philadelphia Story.* Or *The Bitter Tea of General Yen?*

TOM.   Those movies were made in the 1930s.

AMANDA.   They're still good today.

TOM.   I don't want to have this conversation. I'm going to the movies.

AMANDA.   That's right, go to the movies! Don't think about us, a mother alone, an unmarried brother who thinks he's crippled and has no job. *(Sees Lawrence, pokes him.)* Oh, stop holding your breath, Lawrence, mama was kidding. *(Back to Tom.)* Don't let anything interfere with your selfish pleasure. Go see your pornographic trash that's worse than anything Mr. D.H. Lawrence ever envisioned. Just go, go, go — to the movies!

TOM. Alright, I will! And the more you shout about my self-ishness and my taste in movies the quicker I'll go, and I won't just go to the movies!

AMANDA. Go then! Go to the moon — you selfish dreamer! *(Tom exits.)* Oh, Lawrence, honey, what's to become of us?

LAWRENCE. *(Sees Tom's newspaper on the table.)* Tom forgot his newspaper, mama.

AMANDA. He forgot a lot more than that, Lawrence honey. *(Sits on couch next to Lawrence.)* He forgot his mama and brother. *(Lights dim on Amanda and Lawrence on the couch, perhaps with Lawrence's head on Amanda's shoulder. Lights lower to a dim glow on the two of them, as if they are memory. They are still. Tom enters from the side of the stage into a bright spotlight, and addresses the audience directly. His tone is mournful and elegiac.)*

TOM. I didn't go to the moon, I went to the movies. In Amsterdam. A long, lonely trip working my way on a freighter. They had good movies in Amsterdam. They weren't in English, but I didn't really care. And as for my mother and brother — well they were impossible to live with, so I didn't miss them.

Or so I thought. For something pursued me. It always came upon me unawares, it always caught me by surprise. Sometimes it would be a swizzle stick in someone's vodka glass, or sometimes it would just be a jar of pigs feet. But then all of a sudden my brother touches my shoulder, and my mother puts her hands around my neck, and everywhere I look I am reminded of them. And in all the bars I go to there are those damn swizzle sticks everywhere.

I find myself thinking of my brother Lawrence. And of his collection of glass. And of my mother. I begin to think that their story would maybe make a good novel, or even a play. A mother's hopes, a brother's dreams. Pathos, humor, even tragedy. But then I lose interest, I really haven't the energy.

So I'll leave them both, dimly lit, in my memory. For nowadays the world is lit by lightning; and when we get those colored lights going, it feels like I'm on LSD. Or some other drug. Or maybe it's the trick of memory, or the memory of some trick.

Play with your cocktail stirrers, Lawrence. And so, good-bye.

AMANDA. *(Calling over in Tom's direction.)* Tom, I hear you out on the porch talking. Who are you talking to? *(Lights come back up on Amanda and Lawrence.)*

TOM. No one, mother. I'm just on my way to the movies.

AMANDA. Well, try not to be too late, you have to work early at the warehouse tomorrow. And please don't bring home any visitors from the movies, I'm not up to it any after that awful girl. Besides, if some sailor misses his boat, that's no reason you have to put him up in your room. You're too big-hearted, son.

TOM. Yes, mother. See you later. *(Exits.)*

LAWRENCE. *(Holding up a swizzle stick.)* Look at the light through the glass, mama. Isn't it amazin'?

AMANDA. Yes, I guess it is, Lawrence. Oh, but both my children are weird. What have I done, O Lord, to deserve them?

LAWRENCE. Just lucky, mama.

AMANDA. Don't make jokes, Lawrence. Your asthma. Your eczema. My life.

LAWRENCE. Don't be sad, mama. We have each other for company and amusement.

AMANDA. That's right. It's always darkest before the dawn. Or right before a typhoon sweeps up and kills everybody.

LAWRENCE. Oh poor mama, let me try to cheer you up with my collection. Is that a good idea?

AMANDA. It's just great, Lawrence. Thank you.

LAWRENCE. *(Holds up yellow swizzle stick.)* I call this one daffodil, because it's yellow, and daffodils are yellow.

AMANDA. Uh huh.

LAWRENCE. *(Holds up a clear one.)* And I call this one curtain rod because it reminds me of a curtain rod.

AMANDA. Uh huh.

LAWRENCE. *(Holds up a blue one.)* And I call this one ocean, because it's blue, and [the ocean is ...]

AMANDA. I THOUGHT YOU CALLED THE BLUE ONE *BLUE*, YOU IDIOT CHILD! DO I HAVE TO LISTEN TO THIS PATHETIC PRATTLING THE REST OF MY LIFE???

28

CAN'T YOU AT LEAST BE CONSISTENT???

LAWRENCE. *(Shocked; hurt.)* No, I guess, I can't.

AMANDA. *(Still angry.)* Well, *try*, can't you? *(Silence.)* I'm sorry, Lawrence. I'm a little short-tempered today.

LAWRENCE. *(Still hurt.)* That's alright. *(Silence. Amanda looks at Lawrence, and feels bad for yelling at her pathetic child. She decides to try to make up.)*

AMANDA. Do you have any other swizzle sticks with names, Lawrence?

LAWRENCE. Yes, I do. *(Holds one up.)* I call this one "mama." *(Throws it onto the floor with a sudden sharp motion. Pause. Amanda has to take this in.)*

AMANDA. Well, that's lovely, Lawrence, thank you.

LAWRENCE. I guess *I* can be a little short-tempered too.

AMANDA. Yes, well, whatever. *(Deciding to defuse this argument.)* I think we won't kill each other this evening, alright?

LAWRENCE. Alright.

AMANDA. I'll just distract myself from my rage and despair, and read about other people's rage and despair in the newspaper, shall I? *(Picks up Tom's newspaper.)* Your brother has the worst reading and viewing taste of any living creature. This is just a piece of filth. *(Reads.)* Man Has Sex with Chicken, Then Makes Casserole. *(Closes the paper.)* Disgusting. Oh, Lawrence honey, look — it's the *Evening Star. (Holds the paper up above their heads; we see its banner reads* Evening Star.*)* Let's make a wish on it, honey, shall we?

LAWRENCE. Alright, mama. *(Amanda holds up the newspaper, and she and Lawrence close their eyes and make a wish.)*

AMANDA. What did you wish for, darlin'?

LAWRENCE. More swizzle sticks.

AMANDA. You're so predictable, Lawrence. It's part of your charm, I guess.

LAWRENCE. *(Sweetly.)* What did you wish for, mama?

AMANDA. The same thing, honey. *(Wistful.)* Maybe just a little happiness, too ... but mostly just some more swizzle sticks. *(Sad music. Amanda and Lawrence look up at the* Evening Star. *Fade to black.)*

A STYE
OF THE EYE

A STYE OF THE EYE was part of the six-play evening, DURANG/DURANG, produced at Manhattan Theatre Club (Lynne Meadow, Artistic Director; Barry Grove, Managing Director) in New York City on November 14, 1994. It was directed by Walter Bobbie; the set design was by Derek McLane; the costume design was by David C. Woolard; the lighting design was by Brian Nason; the sound design was by Tony Meola; the production stage manager was Perry Cline and the stage manager was Gregg Fletcher. The cast was as follows:

JAKE .... Marcus Giamatti
MA .... Becky Ann Baker
DR. MARTINA .... Patricia Elliott
AGNES/BETH .... Keith Reddin
MEG .... Lizbeth Mackay
WESLEY .... David Aaron Baker
MAE .... Patricia Randell

NOTE: Beth plays "Agnes" in "Agnes is Odd," the play-within-a-play section. Beth is written to be played by the same male actor who plays Lawrence. Even if done on a single bill, it is best when played by a sensitive looking young man rather than by a woman.

A previous version of this play, without the character of Wesley, was presented by the American Repertory Theatre in Cambridge, Massachusetts as part of an evening called MRS. SORKEN PRESENTS. This evening had versions of MRS. SORKEN and STYE in it, but did not have the other four plays in DURANG/DURANG. The cast of STYE at A.R.T. was Thomas Derrah, Pamela Gien, Harriet Harris, Isabell Monk, James Andreassi, Nina Bernstein, Dean Norris.

A STYE
OF THE EYE

A desolate prairie. Wind-swept. Maybe a couple of discarded truck tires piled on one another. Or maybe it's a highway in the midst of a prairie. Anyway, not much scenery. Desolate, isolated, out west somewhere.

On one part of the stage we see Jake, who is on a pay phone. He is tall, in his 30s, and dressed in dungarees, boots and a T-shirt or work shirt. He is masculine, and has a raging temper.

JAKE.   Answer the phone, damn it. Answer the phone. *(Bangs the phone receiver on the side of the phone, or any other surface.)* Come on, come on! *(Into receiver.)* Hello! Hello! *(Lights up on a different part of the stage. Ma is discovered next to a phone, or enters calmly over to the ringing phone. Ma is between 40 and 50, and dressed in a sloppy, comfortable print dress. Her hair is not fussed with, just pulled back out of her face. She is a no-nonsense woman, tough, matter-of-fact, sounds like a Cracker.)*
MA.   Hello?
JAKE.   Hey, Ma?
MA.   Who is this?
JAKE.   Ma, it's your son.
MA.   Who?
JAKE.   Your son, ma.
MA.   I got two sons. Which one are you?
JAKE.   I'm Jake.
MA.   Jake?
JAKE.   Jake!
MA.   You're not the other one? What's his name?

JAKE.   Frankie. No, it's not Frankie, Ma. It's Jake.

MA.   Jake?

JAKE.   Stop saying Jake, or I'm going to come over to your house and punch you in the mouth.

MA.   *(Her voice warming, friendly.)* Oh, now it sounds like Jake. How are you, baby?

JAKE.   She's real bad, Ma.

MA.   Who, Jake?

JAKE.   She's all red and blue and purple.

MA.   Who you talkin' about, Jake?

JAKE.   I had to hit her. She was dressin' real sexy like, and goin' off to rehearsal.

MA.   Who is this you're talkin' about, Jake?

JAKE.   It's Beth, Ma. My wife.

MA.   Are you married, Jake?

JAKE.   Ma, you know I am. You wuz at the wedding.

MA.   Why didn't you marry your sister, Jake, she always liked you.

JAKE.   That would be incest, Ma.

MA.   No, it wouldn't. Incest would be if you married me. If you married your sister, it would be ... sorority.

JAKE.   Shut the fuck up, Ma. I'm tryin' to tell you I killed Beth.

MA.   Who's Beth?

(Note: Ma's lapses in memory are complete. When she says something like "Who's Beth," she has no recollection whatsoever that she heard the name Beth a few seconds before. So all her questions are asked innocently, trying her best to get information. There is no "what was that thing you said a moment ago" tone to any of her repeating questions. And thus when Jake seems irritated with her forgetting, she has no idea what is the cause of his frustration.)

JAKE.   She's my wife.

MA.   I didn't know you were married.

JAKE.   You have the attention span of a gnat. Ma, we've been through this. Beth is my wife, you wuz at the wedding, and I just killed her.

MA.   *(Suspicious.)* Who is this calling me?

JAKE.   It's your son, Ma! I just killed my wife.

MA. Well, I never pay attention to the tramps you start up with. She probably asked for it.

JAKE. She was goin' to rehearsal, Ma. She's into actin', Ma, and she's goes off to fuckin' rehearsal, and every day she dresses more slutty like, and I just know that she's doin' it with some fuckin' actor on her lunch break. And I seen her in a play once. She stank.

MA. *(Upset.)* Whatcha goin' to plays for, baby? I didn't bring you up to spend your time goin' to plays. You're gonna end up like that Sam Shepard boy down the road. Why don't you settle down and marry your sister?

JAKE. Stop talkin' about incest, Ma. I just killed my wife.

MA. Well, did anyone see you?

JAKE. No.

MA. Well, there, you see. Go get a good night's sleep, and in the morning we'll get you another one. Why don't you marry your sis.... Oh, that's right, you don't like that idea. You're stubborn like your father. I hate his guts. I wish he were dead.

JAKE. He is dead, Ma.

MA. Well, good.

JAKE. I didn't want to kill her, Ma, but she asked for it.

MA. Who you talkin' about, baby?

JAKE. Beth, Beth! How many times do I have to say it!

MA. 33. I'm getting bored with this conversation, Jake. Is your good brother Frankie there?

JAKE. What?

MA. Put Frankie on.

JAKE. He's not here.

MA. Put him on.

JAKE. He's not here.

MA. Frankie, is that you?

JAKE. Wait a minute, Ma.

MA. Did you hear what Jake told me?

JAKE. Hold your horses a minute, Ma. Hey, Frankie! Ma wants to speak to you! Frankie! *(Changes personalities, and switches phone hands; sounds more polite and reasoned though still has a temper.)* Hey, Mom, how are you?

MA.   Oh, Frankie, I love it the way you call me "Mom" and Jake calls me "Ma." It's so differentiating. Frankie, did you hear that Jake killed his wife?

JAKE.   He told me, Mom. He's a crazy, spoiled, mixed up kid. If only Pa weren't a drunk and a skunk and dead.

MA.   Is he dead?

JAKE.   You know he's dead. We were all at the funeral, and you spit on his grave.

MA.   Was that your pa? Well, he never was no good. But he sure could ride a horse, and shoot a rifle, and wear boots and dungarees.

JAKE.   Mom, what are we gonna do about Jake?

MA.   Why did I spit on his grave?

JAKE.   I don't know. You wuz angry. Everyone in this family has a fierce temper.

MA.   *(Proudly.)* We do. We're fierce, us Faberizzi's.

JAKE.   Mom, we're not Italian.

MA.   Well, what's our last name then?

JAKE.   We don't have a last name. Mom, what are we going to do about Jake?

MA.   Who?

JAKE.   Jake.

MA.   Jake's dead. His wife just killed him.

JAKE.   You got it backwards, Ma. I mean "Mom."

MA.   You know you and Jake sound so much alike that sometimes I think you're both two different aspects of the same personality. That means I gave birth to a symbol, and me with no college edjacation.

JAKE.   I'm not a symbol, Ma. I'm a westerner looking for the big open expanses, but they're gettin' smaller and smaller. There's no place to hope, Ma.

MA.   You sound like a symbol. But not some prissy Ivy League-type symbol. My children are virile, masculine symbols who carry guns and beat up women. You all got so much testosterone in you, that you got a native kinda poetry in you, even when you spit. Why don't you go kill a woman like your brother?

JAKE.   But what woman is like my brother?

MA.   That's not what I meant, stupid. The verb was implied in that sentence, as in "Why don't you go kill a woman like your brother *did*," "did" in imaginary bracket signs. And me with no college edjacation. Put Jake back on the line, honey, I'm bored with this conversation. No, never mind, I got an idea. Why don't you go try to find Beth. Maybe she's not dead. Maybe she's only brain damaged, and *you* can marry her. That might have symbolic value of some sort.

JAKE.   But what symbolic value would that have, Mom?

MA.   I don't know, I'm not a writer. But if you put some jazz music under it, or some good country sounds, it's bound to mean somethin' to somebody. I gotta go now, Frankie, the cactus is whistlin' on the stove. But you keep an eye on your brother, and if you wanna marry your sister, just let me know. *(Hangs up, exits; lights fade on her part of the stage.)*

JAKE.   Goodbye, Mom. *(Switches to Jake personality; grabs for phone from himself.)* Hey, I ain't done talkin' to her yet! *(Switches back to Frankie, hangs up the phone.)* Well, she's done talkin' to you. Why'd you go and kill her, Jake? *(Switches to Jake.)* Ma? *(Switches to Frankie, annoyed.)* No, not Mom. Beth. *(Switches to Jake.)* I don't know. She just kept goin' to all them rehearsals and ... well, it irritated me. *(Switches to Frankie.)* I can understand that. *(Switches to Jake; vehement.)* Especially this one play called "Agnes is Odd" or some such thing, all about this flaky nun who killed her baby. *(Lights change. We see the play Jake is remembering. Jake either exits or stays on the side and watches with the audience. The sound of Stravinsky-like music, or* Carmina Burana.* *Startling, mysterious, other worldly. Enter Dr. Martina Dysart, in a crisp business suit, smoking three cigarettes, one in her mouth, two in her hands. She takes the one in her mouth out, and addresses the audience. She is intense and concerned, solving a deep mystery.)*

DR. MARTINA.   The baby was discovered in a waste basket with the umbilical cord knotted around its neck. The mother was unconscious, next to the body. The mother was a young

---

* See Special Note on Songs and Recordings on copyright page.

nun called Sister Agnes, Sister Agnes Dei. During the night she had given birth and then seemingly killed her baby. Then she went out to the convent stables and blinded eight horses with a metal crucifix. That much is fact. But she is also a musical genius along the lines of Wolfgang Amadeus Mozart. Furthermore, my life as a psychiatrist is drab and depressing, and even though I think it unappealing that she killed her baby and blinded the horses, still I envy her passion. You wouldn't see *me* getting up in the middle of the night to go down to the stables. And furthermore, I'm a lapsed Catholic who wishes I had her faith, and I wish I had a horse, and I ... wish I was a composer. In short, there are many ideas and subtleties to think about here, so stop rattling your programs and let's move on with it. My first meeting with Agnes, I thought she was brain damaged. *(Enter Sister Agnes, the sensitive nun. Dressed perhaps in the strange white nun's outfit Amanda Plummer wore in the Broadway version of* Agnes of God, *which is the same design Sally Field wore in* The Flying Nun *TV series. Or a more conventional nun outfit is okay too. Jake's wife Beth is playing Sister Agnes. Beth is written to be played by a small, sensitive young man.)*

AGNES. Look, stigmata. *(Agnes holds out her palms, which at first glance have gaping red holes in them. A second later one notices that she seems to be holding red rubber things in her palms, with reddish centers to them.)*

DR. MARTINA. Nonsense, those are plastic Dr. Spock ears. Look, I'll show you. *(Dr. Martina removes the "plastic stigmata" and puts the Dr. Spock ears on her ears. She leaves them there for the rest of the scene.)* People sell these at Halloween. Do you like Halloween, Agnes?

AGNES. Pooh. Pooh.

DR. MARTINA. Pooh. Winnie the Pooh? Do you like Winnie the Pooh?

AGNES. Pooh. Pooh. *Puer. (Last word is pronounced "Pooh-air.")*

DR. MARTINA. *Puer.* That's Latin for boy. Do you like boys, Agnes?

AGNES. Pooh-ella.

DR. MARTINA. Yes, *puella.* Latin for girl. Maybe it's Latin you like. Do you like Latin, Agnes? *Hic, haec, hoc,* and all that.

AGNES. *Puer. Puella. Eck, eck, equus! (Momentarily mimes blinding horses, then pulls herself together again.)*

DR. MARTINA.   Boy, girl, horse. This isn't a very intelligent conversation, Agnes. Don't they make you speak sentences in the convent, Agnes?

AGNES.   Agnes Dei.

DR. MARTINA.   Yes, that's Latin for Lamb of God. *(With a shock of recognition.)* Oh my God, your name is Agnes Dei, isn't ? Good grief, I wonder if that means you're some sort of sacificial lamb to God, and that maybe your giving birth was an immaculate conception, and that the father is God Himself!!! Good Lord, what a shocking idea, oh my mind is running, let me try to breath deeply for a moment. *(Puffs on several of her cigarettes.)* Goodness, what dreadful rubbish I was just speaking. Rather like speaking in tongues. Do you like tongues, Agnes?

AGNES.   We had tongue sandwiches at that convent, and it made all the Sisters menstruate.

DR. MARTINA.   *(Pause.)* I think that's rather an obscene remark you've just made, Agnes. Did you mean to be obscene?

AGNES.   Children should be obscene. And not furred.

DR. MARTINA.   Furred?

AGNES.   Furred like a bird.

DR. MARTINA.   What is the matter with you exactly? Are you a saint or are you brain damaged?

AGNES.   *(Sings, lasciviously.)* Erotic, erotic, put your hands all over my body!

DR. MARTINA.   I see. Well, if you're going to sing, I think I'll go now. By the way, which member of the convent is it who won't let you watch MTV? *(Shudders to herself.)* What a sharp remark of mine. I'm definitely in the right profession.

AGNES.   No do with MTV.

DR. MARTINA.   Of course, it do. Does. That's the kind of song that's sung on MTV.

AGNES.   Noooooooo. Who *sing*, Doctor?

DR. MARTINA.   I forget. That slutty woman who changes her look all the time, what's-her-name ... oh my God, her name is *Madonna*, which means "Mother of God!" *(Agnes has a scream-*

ing fit at this scary coincidence, and falls to the ground rolling around in circles, going "Whoop! Whoop! Whooop!")

AGNES.   Whoop! Whoop! Whoop! Whoop! Whoop! *(Lights fade on Agnes and Dr. Martina, and they exit. Lights back up on Jake.)*

JAKE.   *(As Jake; explaining to Frankie.)* It was after that terrible play that I took Beth out in the parking lot and I beat her to a pulp. "Your play was pretentious!" I said, and then I punched her. "You were unconvincing as a nun, and I didn't know whether you were supposed to be crazy or sane," and then I kicked her in the side. "And I don't like the previous play you wuz in, *The Reluctant Debutante,* either," and then I took her head and I put it under the tire of the Chevrolet, and I dropped it on her. And that's how I killed her.

(Switches to Frankie.) Oh, Jake. The play couldn't have been that bad.

(Switches to Jake.) It was. It was. I fuckin' hated it, man. It made me wanna puke.

(Switches to Frankie.) Yeah, but to kill someone.

(Switches to Jake; big baby, teary.) Oh, Frankie, I miss her already. I wish she was alive so we could go on a second honeymoon together.

(Switches to Frankie.) I got some land in Florida I could sell ya.

(Switches to Jake.) Oh yeah?

(Switches to Frankie.) It's called Glengarry Glen Ross.

(Switches to Jake.) Oh I don't want to go there.

(Switches to Frankie, who now speaks in a fast, staccato rhythm, with a lot of aggressive salesman energy.) Why the fuck not? The place is good. Not great maybe, but what I'm sayin' is, it's good. Not great maybe, but good. That's what I'm sayin'. It may be swamp, it may have bugs, but fuck, Jake, what's perfect? You tell me. No, don't tell me, I'll tell you. It's not great, good. Am I right? Do you understand what I'm sayin'? Should I say it again? What I'm sayin' is, fuck shit piss damn, it ain't half bad. Half good, half bad. You gotta settle. It ain't perfect. Settle. Gotta. You gotta settle. A negotiation. Give and take. You know what I'm sayin'? What I'm sayin' is ...

(Switches to Jake, frustrated and angered by Frankie's irritating sales pitch.) Shut up! I know what you're saying, you sound life-like, granted, but you repeat yourself and you're monotonous, and you're ... insensitive to my upset about my wife. She is dead, you know. I deserve sympathy.

(Switches to Frankie.) Yeah, but you killed her.

(Switches to Jake.) Hmmmmm. I wonder if she's not totally dead.

(Switches to Frankie.) Okay, listen here, Jake, I'm gonna go out across the prairie or the highway or wherever we are, and I'm gonna see if I can find her, and if she's alive or not.

(Switches to Jake.) Hey, Frankie, one more thing. If it turns out she's alive, I don't wanna hear you been doin' it with her.

(Switches to Frankie.) Now, Jake, don't start gettin' crazy on me.

(Switches to Jake; violent.) I don't wanna hear it.

(Switches to Frankie.) Okay, you don't gotta hear it. *(To himself.)* I'll say it real soft.

(Switches to Jake.) Whaddit you say?

(Switches to Frankie.) Nothin', Jake, relax. Nothin'. See ya around.

(Switches to Jake; suspicious, hostile.) See ya. *(They exit. Lights change to another part of the stage. It is the home of Meg, who is Beth's mother. At Manhattan Theatre Club, we set this scene outdoors, in front of Meg's house. There was a screen door that led into the house; and there were tires on the outside yard, which people could sit on, or fall on. It would be easy, with tiny line adjustments, to set this scene inside Meg's house if you preferred that. But my references here are to the "outside" setting. Meg enters the yard through her screen door, which closes behind her. Meg is 35 to 45, blowsily attractive. She is based on the character Ann Wedgeworth played in* Lie of the Mind. *Along these lines, she has red hair, kind of trashy jewelry, tight jeans and boots, and a feminine, off-the-shoulder bright blouse. She is sensual, and has a charming drawl to her speech. She might look like a going-to-seed country western singer.)*

MEG.   My, it's hot in that house today. I need some air. Ooo. *(Sound of a sheep from offstage.)* Baylor? Is that you? (Wesley, a young man in jeans and a T-shirt, comes outside through the screen* *door. He is the son of Meg, and the brother of Beth. He carries two large paper grocery bags. He is spacey, and mysterious. His speech is often lacking in emotion, and he seems to have his own thoughts going on a lot.)* Oh, Mike, I thought you wuz your father.

WESLEY.   The baby sheep has maggots in it. I brung it in the kitchen.

MEG.   That's nice. Where is your father? Is he still out hunting deer?

WESLEY.   I guess so. *(Wesley puts his two grocery bags on the ground.)*

MEG.   He's been hunting deer a long time. 15 years, is it?

WESLEY.   I dunno. I went shoppin'.

MEG.   Oh, that's so thoughtful. Your sister Beth should be comin' home from the hospital any minute — Jake didn't kill her after *Agnes Is Odd,* he just damaged her brain a bit, I meant to tell ya. And I want to make her a nice home-cooked meal. *(Meg starts to empty the two bags. The entire contents are artichokes.)* Oh, an artichoke, how nice. Oh, another one. Oh, another one. Mike, honey, we gotta teach you how to shop better. *(Meg continues to empty artichokes onto the yard, or inside the tires. Wesley just stares.)*

WESLEY.   I think I saw Pop in the hunter's cabin. He didn't got no clothes on.

MEG.   Lord, how many artichokes are there here? *(Suddenly hearing it.)* What did you say about maggots and the kitchen?

WESLEY.   The lamb has maggots. I brung it in the kitchen.

MEG.   Mike, honey, you don't bring a critter with maggots into the kitchen.

WESLEY.   Why is Pop naked in the hunter's cabin?

MEG.   I wonder if your sister Beth even likes artichokes. Oh, I think I hear her now. Beth, honey, is that you? *(Enter Beth, same actor who played Agnes. Beth's head is wrapped in an enormous bandage, and she's in a hospital gown. She also limps, and carries a small suitcase. Due to her brain damage, her speech is peculiar now. She often speaks nonsense syllables, but as if they make sense to her. From time to time, she stares off oddly.)*

BETH.   Monga raga. Luga mee.

MEG.   Oh, Lord, you look awful. Doesn't she look awful,

42

Mike?

WESLEY.   My name is Wesley. *(Exits.)*

MEG.   Oh Beth honey, the doctors said you had brain damage. Is that right?

BETH.   *(Greeting her mother, telling of her recent experiences.)* Mummy. Mommy. Custom. Costume. Capsule. Cupcake. Candle. Campbell. Chunky Beef Soup. Ugga wugga meatball.

MEG.   Oh! Well, that made sense. Mike, she's makin' sense to me. *(Enter Jake.)*

JAKE.   Is Beth still alive?

MEG.   Oh my God, he's come to finish her off! Mike, do somethin'.

BETH.   *(Excited to see him.)* Jake? Joke? Kill me, joke? Jake?

JAKE.   I'm not Jake, Beth. I'm his good brother Frankie.

BETH.   Jake? I want Jake.

MEG.   Goodness, he nearly killed her, and she wants him. Isn't the human heart peculiar?

JAKE.   *(To Meg.)* I'm sorry about what my brother did to your daughter, ma'am, and I hope you don't mind my comin' here.

MEG.   Oh, an apology. Oh my. *(Cries. Enter Wesley. He's only wearing underpants now, and untied work boots. He has two more bags of groceries, also with artichokes. He puts them down on the ground, and exits.)* Oh good, more artichokes.

BETH.   Jake?

JAKE.   No, Beth, I'm Frankie.

BETH.   I want Jake.

MEG.   No, honey. Jake plays too rough.

BETH.   Need. Bleed. I am a Jake Junkie.

MEG.   *(Sound of lamb bleating.)* Mike, I hope you're getting that lamb outta the kitchen, honey.

BETH.   *(Sudden fear; feeling of significance.)* Lamb? Lamb of God? *Agnus Dei?*

MEG.   What? I guess so, honey. *(Enter Wesley.)*

WESLEY.   Do we have any mint jelly?

MEG.   I don't know, honey. Have you said hello to your sister Beth?

WESLEY.   No. *(Exits back into house.)*

BETH.   *(To Jake.)* Jelly. Junket. Jacket. Jake.

43

JAKE. I'm not Jake, Beth. I'm Frankie.

BETH. Frankie? Funky. Fatty. Patty. Head wooound.

MEG. Oh, it's going to be hard to cast her in plays now. No Restoration comedy for you, young lady!

JAKE. I just wanted to see that you were alright, Beth.

BETH. Wait. Love. Life. The Call of the Wild. Coyote. Aawoooooooooooooo! I want to marry you.

JAKE. But you already have a husband. You're married to my brother.

BETH. You be my husband. I be your wife. You be, I be, we be.

MEG. She's so much more interesting to listen to since her accident, isn't she? And a wedding, what a good idea. Excuse me, I want to see if there are maggots in the kitchen. Mike! *(Exits.)*

BETH. We become one together, Frankie, and we make a baby out of paper mâché maybe. Baby maybe.

JAKE. I'm in love with you, Beth, but I feel such guilt at betraying my brother. *(Enter Mae, Jake's sister. She wears a tight, sexy red dress, and stands provocatively.)*

MAE. And what about betraying your sister?

BETH. Oooh, pretty dress.

MAE. Here, you can try it on. *(Mae takes off her dress, and gives it to Beth, who runs happily into the house with it, very excited. Mae is now dressed in an attractive slip, and high heels. Jake and Mae kiss passionately, then rush to opposite sides of the room, banging into the walls, or sides of the stage.)*

JAKE. Why'd you come here, Mae?

MAE. I can't get you outta my head, Jake. You run around my brain like a haunting refrain. I love ya.

JAKE. I'm not Jake. I'm Frankie.

MAE. Oh, ain't you realized yet, you're two aspects of the same personality. And you and I are two aspects of the same personality, only we're male and female, and you're male and male, so I wish you'd get yourself into one person so you and I could combine into one person also. But if you remain two people, then when you and I combine, we'll be three people, and that's not what I want.

JAKE. What?

MAE. I can't say that all again. What part didn't you hear?

JAKE. Mae. *(They rush from opposite sides of the yard and embrace. She beats his chest. They roll about on the floor. They are very passionate.)* How'd you know where to find me?

MAE. Ma tol' me.

JAKE. Ma. She's a sick lady.

MAE. Do you know how to spell Mae? You spell it just like Ma, but add an "e" to it.

JAKE. What the hell's that supposed to mean?

MAE. I don't know. *(They run from opposite sides again, and embrace passionately. Meg enters.)*

MEG. Sorry to interrupt, but I have something to tell you. *(Points to her eye.)* I have a stye in my eye. And it hurts when I close my eye and see nothing, and it hurts when I open my eye and look around. No matter what I do it hurts. This stye in my eye is a symbol. I have a symbol in my eye. *(Smiles.)* I just wanted you to know. *(Exits back into house.)*

MAE. I was in the school orchestra in Texas when I first started to lust after you, Jake, and you know what instrument I played? The cymbals.

JAKE. We come together like two cymbals crashing, don't we, Mae?

MAE. Yes. Let's you run to that side of the yard, and I'll run to the other side, and then we'll run together again.

JAKE. *(Excited.)* Okay. *(They run to opposite sides. Just as they are about to run together, enter Beth, now dressed in Mae's red dress, but with lots of jangly jewelry and a purse, purple stockings, high heels, and a strange, teased wig. It is a demented person's attempt to look attractive. She kind of looks like "Carnaby Street" London fashions of the 60s, which is most incongruous for this prairie setting.)*

BETH. I feel like the jewelry counter at Woolworth's.

JAKE. You look like the jewelry counter at Woolworth's. *(Enter Meg, carrying an American flag. She now wears an eye patch over her eye with the stye in it.)*

MEG. I found this nice flag in the kitchen. I think it's American. *(Sees Beth.)* Oh, don't you look nice? When's the wedding?

MAE. What wedding?

JAKE.   I told Beth I'd marry her.

(Switches to Jake.) Frankie! What did you say? I thought so! The minute I turn out not to have killed her, the two of you try to betray me!

(Switches to Frankie.) Now, Jake, stay calm.

(Switches to Jake.) I can't stay calm. You been doin' it with my wife.

(Switches to Frankie.) We ain't done it yet, Jake.

(Switches to Jake.) Yeah, but you were gonna! Yippie-i-o-ki-ay, that makes me mad! I'm gonna have to take out my gun, Frankie!

(Switches to Frankie; in fear for his life.) Don't take out that gun. Jake! Jake! Don't shoot me! I'm your brother! Jake! *(Sound of a gun shot. Jake falls to the ground, dead.)*

MAE.   He's dead. Jake shot him.

MEG.   *Who* shot him? I didn't follow that visually at all. Maybe it's because of the stye in my eye. Oh dear, I think I'm developing a stye in my other eye. *(The eye patch Meg is wearing on her eye is a double one, and she moves the top one over to cover her remaining eye. She now has eye patches on both of her eyes.)* Oh, Lord, I can't see anything now.

MAE.   Jake, Frankie. Jake, Frankie. We can't be one together. Now I'm just half. Or three-fifths. I need two-fifths.

BETH.   *(Chipper.)* Well, I don't care. These clothes make me want to go back on the stage. Goodbye, mother. Goodbye, Jake. I'm going to star with RuPaul and Charles Busch in Edward Albee's *Three Tall Women*. In Act Two, I get to be in a coma. Goodbye! *(Beth exits.)*

MEG.   She really is brain damaged. *(Enter Ma.)*

MA.   Hi, everybody. I was just on my way to work at the Roy Rogers chain of restaurants, I'm the French fries girl, when I set my house on fire and decided to come on over here for a nice little set-down and heigh-ho, how are ya?

MEG.   Oh, you're just in time to help me fold the American flag.

MA.   What American flag? *(Meg and Ma start to try to fold the American flag.)*

MEG.   I found it in the kitchen. I hope it doesn't have mag-

46

gots in it.

MA. Maggots in the flag? Oh. That sounds serious.

MAE. Do you have any cymbals in the house? Oh, there they are. *(Mae gets a pair of cymbals easily from somewhere hidden on the stage; at Manhattan Theatre Club they were inside the two tires. To the dead body of Jake.)* Jake, Frankie. Do you remember that song we used to play in high school? *(Sings.)*

Blue moon,
It hangs up high in the sky,

(Bangs the cymbals. Sings.)

Without a dream in my heart,
Without a stye in my eye …

(Bangs the cymbals.)

I love you, Jake, Frankie. I'm desperate without you. *(Enter Wesley. His underpants are now splattered with some blood. Not too gross, but noticeable.)*

WESLEY. The baby lamb is dead.

MEG. Well, please get it out of the kitchen. *(To Ma.)* I'm sorry. Do you know my son Mike?

WESLEY. My name's Wesley.

MA. How ya doin'? I like your bloody underpants. Oooh. Something's wrong with my eyes.

MEG. Are you developing styes?

MA. Don't think so. I think I'm going blind. *(Puts on dark glasses.)*

MEG. Well, we'll just have to fold the flag as best we can.

MA. Alrighty-dighty. *(Meg, with her two eye patches, and Ma, with her dark glasses, try to fold the flag some more. It's not easy for them.)*

MAE. You're blind, and you're folding the American flag.

WESLEY. There are maggots in the American flag. Pop is naked in the hunter's cabin. The baby lamb is dead.

MAE. Why does all this information make me want to crash the cymbals again? *(Crashes her cymbals. Jake stands.)*

JAKE. Would you stop that God-awful racket? *(Stands, brushes himself off.)* I'm sorry I killed Frankie, but maybe I can be free now that he's dead. Did I kill Beth too?

MAE. Beth has gone back to theatre.

47

JAKE. That's a kind of death. (*Jake looks out. A lone jazz instrument plays in the background. Moody, yearning. The characters notice the sound of the jazz.*) I'm gonna go out west and look for open spaces. I've been lookin' for love in all the wrong places. I'm sick of women.

MEG. Well, I certainly think Beth was a transvestite anyway. (*Jazz music fades out.*) I always presumed that's why you beat her up. Or maybe I'm the transvestite. Oh, we forget the things we don't want to remember. That's a theme of the play. Oh the meaning, the meaning. Who am I talkin' to?

JAKE. Me, but I want to talk again. (*Jazz music starts up again.*) I'm sick of women. I'm gonna find me some Mexican whores and some tequila, and I'm gonna drive me down some highway with open spaces on either side of me and I'm gonna sit in the car with my legs spread open real wide so my peter can breath, and I'm gonna live like a real man, away from civilization and from styes in the eye. (*Exits to his new life; jazz music fades out.*)

MAE. He's gone. Love and hate is mixed up in my heart. What'll we do?

MA. We got to stick together. We got to go back to our roots. We got to get our heads examined.

WESLEY. I want to have a speech.

MEG. Honey, we gotta wrap this thing up. Make it short.

WESLEY. Could I have jazz music please? (*Jazz starts again.*) Artichokes. There are three different words in "artichoke." There's "art." And there's "choke." And there's "ih."

MAE. What does that mean?

MA. You're the one holding the cymbals, not him.

MAE. I don't think they are cymbals.

MEG. No?

MAE. I think ... they represent somethin' else.

MEG. I wonder ... if they're connected to ... (*Importantly, mysteriously.*) ... the styes in my eye. (*Everyone looks out in the distance, and stares importantly. Lights dim. The sound of wind whistling through the prairie. A coyote's howl is heard. End of play.*)

NINA IN
THE MORNING

NINA IN THE MORNING was part of the six-play evening, DURANG/DURANG, produced at Manhattan Theatre Club (Lynne Meadow, Artistic Director; Barry Grove, Managing Director) in New York City on November 14, 1994. It was directed by Walter Bobbie; the set design was by Derek McLane; the costume design was by David C. Woolard; the lighting design was by Brian Nason; the sound design was by Tony Meola; the production stage manager was Perry Cline and the stage manager was Gregg Fletcher. The cast was as follows:

NARRATOR..David Aaron Baker
THE MAID .... Patricia Randell
NINA .... Patricia Elliott
JAMES/ROBERT/LA-LA ....Keith Reddin
FOOTE .... Marcus Giamatti

NOTE: The Maid is an optional part. She has no lines, but you may choose to add her presence for ambience and to help Foote carry his various props. And the children of Nina — James, Robert, and La-La — are written to be played by one actor.

NINA IN
THE MORNING

A beautiful room in a rather elaborate household — a cha-teau, a small castle? At Manhattan Theatre Club they had floor-to-ceiling sheer curtains in front of a beautiful azure blue scrim. The sound of the ocean. The curtains gently move to a breeze.

There is a beautiful chaise. And in front of the chaise, a tall, gilt-edged mirror.

The mirror should be only a frame, with nothing where the mirror glass itself would be. Thus an actor can sit or stand behind it, and still be seen by the audience. Seeing a reflec-tion in the mirror is mimed.

Beautiful, mysterious music is heard. A lovely, haunting so-prano aria perhaps.

The Narrator is onstage. He is dressed in a tuxedo and looks elegant.

As the music is finishing, Nina enters.

She is dressed beautifully. (At MTC the designer put her in an off-the-shoulder red gown, with a very very long train. However she is dressed, it should be elegant and flattering to the actress. And a little extreme.)

Her age is indeterminate — definitely over 40 though — and her face is on the white side, with perhaps too much make-

up. She walks towards her chaise with great regalness, as if she's in a procession, on her way to be crowned.

When the Narrator speaks, he is speaking her thoughts, usually. So her facial expressions change with his comments. She does not otherwise look at him or relate to him (with a couple of noted exceptions).

NARRATOR.   The mist hangs heavy over the ocean today. Nina woke from an uncertain sleep and walked to the chaise in her dressing room and sat in front of the beautiful, cherished mirror. *(Nina sits on her chaise, and looks out to her mirror and gasps.)* Her facelift had fallen during the night, and her cheeks were held in place by straight pins.

NINA.   *(Looking in mirror, touching her face delicately.)* Oh, Lord. Oh, Lord. How dreadful. *(Enter James, her child, dressed in short pants and a white shirt. He looks like a well-dressed prep school boy. Played by an actor somewhere in his 20s or young-looking 30s.)*

JAMES.   Good morning, mother.

NINA.   Don't kiss mommy today, her face is precarious.

JAMES.   I don't want to kiss you anyway. I hate you.

NINA.   Please don't upset me, James. My plastic surgeon is in Aruba.

JAMES.   What's this pin for? *(Reaches for her face, pulls out a pin.)*

NINA.   James, stop that. Stop it. Foote! Foote! Come quickly, James is at my face again.

NARRATOR.   But James kept reaching for Nina's face, over and over.

NINA.   Stop it, you unruly child. *(James keeps trying to pull pins out of her face. Nina keeps trying to protect her face. All the pin business is mimed. Foote, the family manservant, enters. He is dignified and in a tuxedo.)*

FOOTE.   You called, Madame?

JAMES.   I want to pull your face off, mother!

NARRATOR.   Foote, seeing Nina's predicament with her son, pulled James away from her, pushed him to the ground, and sat on him. (*Foote pulls James away, pushes him on the ground and sits on him.*)

NINA.   Gently, Foote, gently.

JAMES.   (*Struggling under Foote.*) I hate you, mother, I hate you.

NARRATOR.   Foote took out a hypodermic from his jacket pocket, and gave the misbehaving child a shot. (*Foote does all that.*)

JAMES.   I hate you. I'm sleepy. (*Passes out.*)

FOOTE.   Will that be all, Madame?

NARRATOR.   Foote was the family manservant, and often gave the children general anesthesia whenever they became unruly. Foote had once been a dentist.

NINA.   Thank you, Foote. James was pulling pins out again. I must have done something wrong raising them. I thought I often smiled. I wonder if they wanted anything else.

FOOTE.   Do you wish me to remove any teeth while he's out?

NINA.   No, no. Leave his teeth alone, Foote. I just want quiet for a while. Look at how peaceful James is, curled on the floor. I always liked my children best when they were unconscious.

FOOTE.   If Madame needs me further, just call.

NINA.   Thank you, Foote. You're a jewel. (*Foote exits.*)

NARRATOR.   Foote withdrew, leaving Nina with her thoughts. She thought about her face. She thought about James. Psychotherapy had been no help for James except perhaps in helping him to express his anger more freely, and how useful had that been.

NINA.   (*Sort of to herself.*) Not very.

NARRATOR.   Nina's hands shook as she lifted a coffee cup to her face. Her perceptions were off, and she poured hot liquid down the left side of her face. She put cream and sugar on her face, stirred it, and then rang the bell for Foote. (*Nina mimes the actions the Narrator says above while, or shortly after, he says them. She uses a real cup, spoon, cream pitcher, and sugar bowl, but no actual liquids or sugar. She does all the gestures without emotion. She feels the heat of the coffee and the mess of the liquids <u>after</u> she has done all of them. Then she makes a face of pain, and con-*

fusion. Then she rings the bell.)

NINA.   Foote, I need you. Bring a wet cloth. I'm sticky.

NARRATOR.   Foote brought a basin of warm water and a roll of gauze and sponged her gingerly. *(Foote enters with a Maid as the Narrator speaks. The Maid has a tray with a silver bowl and a gauze. Foote starts to pat Nina's face lightly with the cloth.)*

NINA.   Do you think I'm beautiful, Foote?

FOOTE.   You once were very striking, Madame.

NINA.   Yes, but now, what do you think of me now?

FOOTE.   *(Looks at her.)* You have a quite a nasty burn on your face, Madame. Would you care for a shot of Novocain?

NINA.   Go away, Foote. I want to think.

NARRATOR.   And again, Foote withdrew, dragging James after him. *(Foote drags James out the door, while the Maid curtsies and follows after them.)* Nina racked her brain, trying to remember what she wanted to think. The colors of her wall were beige. She had wanted burnt orange, but the designer had run through the house screaming "Beige! Beige!" and they finally had to give him his way.

NINA.   *(Out, to the imagined designer.)* I wanted burnt orange, but you have given me beige.

NARRATOR.   Later the designer turned against her too, like her son James. No, no, Nina wanted pleasant thoughts, nice things. Flowers, butterflies …

NINA.   *(Hopefully.)* Little duckies.

NARRATOR.   *The Little Prince* by Saint-Exupery. That was a nauseating little book, she had never finished it. Some monk gave it to her when her car had been stopped at a traffic light. *(The Narrator sits stiffly at the bottom of the chaise. He holds his arms as if holding a steering wheel. He stands in for the chauffeur now.)*

NINA.   Drive on, Lance.

NARRATOR.   *(To the audience.)* But Lance, the handsome chauffeur, insisted on the necessity of obeying the red light. *(Speaking as Lance, to Nina.)* "I must obey the red light, Madame."

NINA.   Laws are for other people, Lance. Not for me.

NARRATOR.   *(Speaking as Lance.)* "I'm sorry, Madame. I don't

54

wish to lose my license."

NINA.   I said, drive on, Lance.

NARRATOR.   *(To the audience again.)* But the Mercedes just sat there, and the monk had a chance to pass the stupid book through the car window. *(A Monk scurries across the stage, stopping just long enough to drop a copy of* The Little Prince *on Nina's chaise-car. He then scurries the rest of the way off.)*

NINA.   Kill that monk, Lance.

NARRATOR.   *(To audience.)* But Lance was selective in what commands of hers he followed, and eventually he had to be fired. *(The Narrator stands, no longer playing Lance. He returns to his narration role.)* A long succession of chauffeurs followed, none satisfactory. Finally she gave up riding in the car. She stayed at home, hoping for visitors. *(Nina rings the bell. Foote appears immediately, and waits for her bidding.)*

NINA.   Foote, if any Jehovah's Witnesses come today, show them in, will you? *(Foote exits.)*

NARRATOR.   But no Jehovah's Witnesses came. And Nina found she had to fill the time with thinking, and reminiscing. Nina had once been beautiful.

NINA.   I am very beautiful.

NARRATOR.   Men would stop on the street to stare at her. She caused traffic accidents. Jealous women would rush up to her in their homeliness and try to kill her.

NINA.   Homely women were always trying to shoot me. It was flattering really.

NARRATOR.   Everywhere she went, her eyes would anxiously seek out the mirrors. Sometimes she would bring her own mirrors with her.

NINA.   Put this up, would you?

NARRATOR.   ... Nina would say, lugging a large mirror, and few could deny her. Her love affairs were unpredictable and random. Sometimes it would be royalty, other times it would be the men from the electric company. *(The Narrator turns his back, pretending to look at a power box. He is now the electric company man. Nina comes up to him, stands close and seductive.)*

NINA.   I don't really know where the power box is, I'm afraid. Would you care to lie down? *(The Narrator reverts to his*

Narrator role, and addresses the audience again.)

NARRATOR.   Sometimes when she was especially lonely, she would try to seduce her children. *(James enters, dressed as before as a prep school boy. He, though, also carries a tin lunch box. He sits on the chaise and looks at Nina.)*

NINA.   Don't you find mommy especially attractive today?

NARRATOR.   She would ask James ... *(James looks startled.)* ... and Robert ... *(The actor playing James puts on black-rimmed glasses, and becomes Robert. His posture changes, and he looks at Nina also surprised, but somehow more adult, more jaded.)* ... and occasionally poor La-La. *(The actor now opens the lunch box, takes out a simple skirt that wraps around in one gesture; and clips a large yellow bow in his hair. He has become LA-LA.)*

LA-LA.   *(Happily and monotonously singing to herself.)* La-la-la-la-la, la-la-la-la, la, la, la, la.... *(The actor finishes his costume change and sits back down; and with a rather foolish and sweetly imbecilic expression, he stares at Nina.)*

NARRATOR.   La-la was retarded, and Nina hated her.

NINA.   *(Firmly.)* La-La! Pay attention! *(La-la turns away, opens up her lunch box and starts looking through it happily.)*

LA-LA.   La-la-la-la-la, la-la-la ...

NINA.   Uhhh. You're *willfully* retarded.

NARRATOR.   Nina would shout this at La-la, and then hit her. *(Nina swats La-la's head. La-La hits her head on the tin lunch box, and sort of stumbles offstage, happy but disoriented.)* But Nina mustn't think of the past now. The present was what held promise. Her plastic surgeon was due back in several days. *(Nina rings the bell.)*

NINA.   *(Grandly.)* Foote, I want a cruller!

NARRATOR.   She heard what she presumed were Foote's footsteps, but they belonged to her second son Robert, who fired two shots, one of which grazed her shoulder. *(Enter Robert, dressed the same as James but with the addition of the glasses. He shoots a pistol twice at his mother. On the second shot, Nina moves her shoulder as if hit.)*

ROBERT.   I hate you, mother!

NARRATOR.   Then he ran into the garden. *(Robert runs off. Nina holds her shoulder and rings the bell again.)*

NINA. Foote, bring the gauze again, please.

NARRATOR. Nina had been presented to the Queen twice. *(Nina forgets her pain, and re-enters memory again. She lets go of her shoulder, and stands proudly to meet the Queen. Then during the following, Nina moves back to her chaise, and Robert enters and sits close to his mother.)* It had been shortly after the second presenting that Nina, having been spurned by a member of the Royal Guard on duty, successfully seduced Robert, who was fifteen and seemed to enjoy the activity for a while but then became hysterical. *(Nina and Robert lean in as if to kiss; suddenly Robert starts to scream hysterically. He stands up upset, looks at her, then screams again, running off. Nina looks after him, unconcerned, quizzical, incomplete.)* The school psychologists were highly critical of Nina's behavior, but she was uninterested in their judgments. And then when Louis Malle made *Murmur of the Heart* she called them up and said:

NINA. There you see! The critics thought it was charming, so I don't know what all the fuss was about *my* behavior.

NARRATOR. Nina quite liked the film, which had to do with a mother seducing her son one afternoon, but she felt that the actress Lea Massari was more coarse-grained than she was.

NINA. My features are more delicate, more lovely. I thought Lea Massari was a bit too earthy. I may be sensual, but I am never earthy.

NARRATOR. Neither Robert nor James would agree to see the film, but La-la sort of liked it. *(Enter La-La, happy, in her own world.)*

LA-LA. La-la-la-la-la, la-la la-la la-la ... *(La-La sits next to Nina and, as if they're watching a movie, stares out with a scrunched up, interested face.)*

NINA. *(To audience.)* Yes, La-la loved the movies. *Murmur of the Heart* she liked. And that other Louis Malle film about suicide, *The Fire Within.* And that early Jeanne Moreau film where she makes love in the bathtub, *The Lovers.* Also directed by Louis Malle. La-la really seemed to like the films of Louis Malle.... *(La-La leans forward in particular concentration.)* ... which just goes to show she's only retarded when she wants to be. No retarded child is going to like the films of Louis

Malle. So I've proved my point, La-La is willfully retarded. *(Nina pushes La-La away; La-La meanders off. Nina's thoughts return to the present, and her wounded shoulder.)* Where is Foote with that gauze, my shoulder is bleeding. Foote! Foote!

NARRATOR.   James' father had been a tax lawyer, but Robert's father had been one of twenty men; and La-la's father had been one of fifty-six men that busy summer she had the beach house painted. After a brief burst of self-judgment, she searched the thesaurus for alternatives to the word "promiscuity."

NINA.   *(Miming looking in a dictionary.)* Synonyms include "debauchery." "Salacity." And "lubricity." "Lubricity." "Loooobricity." "Loooooo-briiiiiiii-ci-teeeeeeeeeeee."

NARRATOR.   Nina liked the sound of "lubricity" and that summer she would climb up the ladders and whisper the word into the house painters' ears. *(The Narrator finds himself near Nina. She stands and seductively whispers in his ear, as if he's the house painter.)*

NINA.   *(Whispering into his ear.)* Lubricity. *(Enter Foote with some more gauze.)*

FOOTE.   Has Madame been shot? *(Nina's thoughts return to the present, and Robert's recent attack on her.)*

NINA.   Yes, Foote. Robert said something to me, something mean, and then he shot me. What took you so long?

FOOTE.   I'm sorry, Madame. I was giving La-La a hypodermic shot to calm her down. She was complaining about something and acting retarded, and now she's quiet and good as a lamb.

NINA.   She is good as a lamb. *(Suddenly remembering; stern.)* Foote. I asked for a cruller. How many times must I ask for a thing before I get it?

FOOTE.   We don't have any crullers. Would you like sausages?

NINA.   Go away, Foote.

FOOTE.   Sorry, Madame. I'll ask Cook to bake some crullers for tomorrow morning.

NINA.   Tomorrow morning? Tomorrow, and tomorrow, and tomorrow. Who knows if I'll want a cruller tomorrow, Foote. It doesn't matter. Leave me now, please.

FOOTE. Yes, Madame. *(Foote exits.)*

NINA.   Oh my life, my life, my life. What has become of my life? *(Looks in the mirror anew.)* And what has become of my face? Oh my. Pins are for curtains, not for faces.

NARRATOR.   Nina stared at herself in the mirror and tried to decide whether or not to kill herself. She stared a long while. She didn't look well. Slowly she took the pins out of her face. *(Nina mimes taking pins out. Then she pulls her cheeks downward, and stares tragically at herself in the mirror.)* Her cheeks drooped downward, and her eyes filled with tears. She looked like Simone Signoret. Late Simone Signoret. Of course, when the doctor returned from Aruba, he'd make Nina look substantially better. And she didn't know how to kill herself, unless one of her children shot her. She rang for Foote. *(Nina rings the bell.)*

NINA.   *(Without force; slipping into despair.)* Foote. Foote.

NARRATOR.   In lieu of crullers, Nina decided to have sausages and general anesthesia. And if Robert shot her while was she was passed out, so be it; and if she woke from her sleep, she'd have a proper lunch.

NINA.   Yes. Death or lunch. Death or lunch. One of the two. *(Nina continues to look in the mirror, touching her face lightly. Lights dim. End.)*

WANDA'S VISIT

WANDA'S VISIT was part of the six-play evening, DURANG/ DURANG, produced at Manhattan Theatre Club (Lynne Meadow, Artistic Director; Barry Grove, Managing Director) in New York City on November 14, 1994. It was directed by Walter Bobbie; the set design was by Derek McLane; the costume design was by David C. Woolard; the lighting design was by Brian Nason; the sound design was by Tony Meola; the production stage manager was Perry Cline and the stage manager was Gregg Fletcher. The cast was as follows:

JIM .... Marcus Giamatti
MARSHA .... Lizbeth Mackay
WANDA .... Becky Ann Baker
WAITER .... David Aaron Baker

NOTE: The characters of TWO HENCHMEN appear briefly at the end of the play. At MTC they were played by Keith Reddin and Patricia Randell (who dressed as a man). I prefer that you not list these parts in the program, however, so that the audience does not expect these characters to appear.

WANDA'S VISIT

A comfortable home in Connecticut. Not realistically designed, though — different areas represent different rooms: the living room, the dining room, the bathroom, the kitchen. The dining room table later doubles as a table in a restaurant.

The furniture and the colors are tastefully chosen. A "country" feel. (At Manhattan Theatre Club the setting was very simple: a round table and three chairs. When the chairs were one way, it was the living room. When the chairs were around the table, it was the dining room. For the bedroom, two chairs were put together and the actors sat on them and spread a comforter over themselves. The bathroom was defined by a square of light.)

This is the home of Jim and Marsha. They enter and come to speak to the audience.

They are attractive, in their mid-to-late 30s. He's in somewhat preppy relaxed clothes — khaki pants, a button-down shirt. She's in a comfortable skirt and blouse, with warm but pale colors. Her hair maybe pulled back.

Their manner in talking to the audience is that of telling a story, but also, perhaps, of explaining themselves to a marriage counselor.

JIM.   Our lives had been seeming dull for a while. You know, nothing major, just sometimes being quiet at dinner.
MARSHA.   After 13 years, you run out of things to say, I guess. Or else it's a phase.
JIM.   I think it's a phase.

MARSHA.   Me too. It'll pass.

JIM.   We've been married for 13 years.

MARSHA.   Our anniversary was in March.

JIM.   So in March we went to dinner and tried to get drunk, but we just got sleepy.

MARSHA.   We didn't try to get drunk.

JIM.   I did.

MARSHA.   We had a very nice time, but the wine made us sleepy.

JIM.   We were in bed at 10:30. Asleep in bed.

MARSHA.   Well, we were tired.

JIM.   And then the next week I got this letter from this old classmate of mine.

MARSHA.   Wanda. He'd never mentioned her.

JIM.   Well, she was just some girl friend. You know. High school.

MARSHA.   Wanda.

JIM.   And Wanda wrote me, saying she'd like to visit. And I asked Marsha if she'd mind.

MARSHA.   I have trouble saying no, most women do, I think. It's not pleasing or something. Anyway, Jim got this letter ...

JIM.   ... and Wanda said she was going to be in our neck of the woods...

MARSHA.   ... and I hate the phrase "neck of the woods"...

JIM.   And I asked you if you'd mind, and you said, it would be fine.

MARSHA.   Well, I have trouble saying no. You know that. You should have said "are you sure" or "really" or something.

JIM.   *(Stymied; out to audience.)* Well, I didn't. I thought it would be fun. You know, to mull over the old high school days — the prom, the high school paper — I was editor ...

MARSHA.   And really, what a ball for me ...

JIM.   And Marsha didn't seem to mind. I mean I can't be a mind-reader. So I wrote Wanda back, and told her we'd love to have her visit. I mean, really it might have been fun. In high school Wanda had been quite a looker.

MARSHA.   And, of course, what an enticement for me. To meet an old high school fantasy. Lucky me.

JIM.   So we set a date, and Marsha cleaned the house and baked a chicken.

MARSHA.   Jim refuses to cook or clean.

JIM.   I mow the lawn, you make the chicken.

MARSHA.   We're old-fashioned, I guess.

JIM.   And so we waited for her visit. *(Lights change. Sound of a car driving up, stopping, and a door slamming.)* Oh, I'll go, honey. It must be Wanda. *(Jim goes off to greet Wanda. Marsha straightens up things one last time. Offstage we hear great whooping and enthusiastic cries of "Jim! Jim!" Marsha looks startled, curious. Wanda and Jim come into the room. Wanda is also mid-to-late 30s, but unlike Jim and Marsha, she is not in as good shape. Her clothes are a little gaudy, her hair looks odd or messy, and she carries a sense of emotional disarray with her. But she also looks kind of fun and colorful.)*

WANDA.   *(With longing.)* Jim!!! *(Wanda throws her arms around Jim with great abandon, and then holds this embrace as if her life depended on it. Marsha goes closer to them, and waits patiently for the appropriate moment to be introduced. Still embracing him.)* Jim. Jim. Oh, Jim, Jim.

MARSHA.   *(Since the embrace doesn't seem to be ending.)* Hello. I'm Marsha, Jim's wife.

WANDA.   *(Breaking from the embrace.)* Oh, hello. Nice to see you. I was just so excited at seeing this guy. Hey, guy. Hey. How ya doin'?

JIM.   I'm fine. *(A little uncertain he recognizes her.)* Wanda?

WANDA.   Are you expecting someone else?

JIM.   No, it's just — well, didn't you used to be blond?

WANDA.   Yeah, and I didn't used to be fat either — although I'm not really fat, my woman's group doesn't let me say that, I just have a food problem and some of it shows. But really I just lost 20 pounds. You should have seen me last month.

JIM.   You seem quite thin.

WANDA.   Oh, you're sweet. I may look thin, but I'm really fat. *(To Marsha.)* Do you have anything I can eat?

MARSHA.   Well …

WANDA.   No, I'm just kidding, it was a joke, it seemed like this set-up, you know, I talk about my weight, and then I say, can I have some food.

MARSHA. But if you're hungry ...

WANDA. *I am not hungry. (Glares at Marsha; then becomes friendly again; to Jim.)* Say, Jim, I love your wife. She reminds me of my mother. *(To Marsha.)* No, no, the positive side of my mother. Really. I like both of you.

MARSHA. Thank you. I like both of you.

WANDA. What?

MARSHA. *(Trying to fix what she said.)* I like you, and I like Jim.

WANDA. You better, you're married to Jim, you lucky dog, you. Oh, give me another hug, guy. *(Wanda gives Jim another bear hug.)* Hrrrrrrrrrrrrrrr.

JIM. Why don't we go in the living room? *(Wanda careens into the living room area, looks around her. They follow.)*

WANDA. Oh, I love this room. It's so "country." Did you do it, Marsha?

MARSHA. Well, we bought the furniture. I never thought of it as "doing it" actually.

WANDA. Oh, it's wonderful. And I should know, because I have terrible taste.

MARSHA. What?

WANDA. I mean I can evaluate good taste in others because I have such bad taste in all my own choices. For instance, my house looks like the interior of a Baskin Robbins. Everything is plastic, and there are all these bright yellows and dark chocolates. Really the only thing worse than being married to me is to have me decorate your house.

JIM. Well, I'm sure you underestimate yourself, Wanda.

WANDA. Isn't he a dreamboat? You're a dreamboat, dreamboat. Well, say, thank you!

JIM. *(Embarrassed.)* Thank you.

WANDA. *(To Marsha; with sudden focus.)* Do you have any-thing to eat? Pretzels or something?

MARSHA. Well, dinner should be ready soon.

WANDA. Oh, Lord, I don't want dinner yet. Just some pret-zels would be good. Something to munch on.

MARSHA.   Would you like some paté?

WANDA.   Pate? *(To Jim.)* Where'd you get her, honey, the back of *The New Yorker?* *(To Marsha.)* Sure, honey, I can eat paté, as long as you have crackers with it. And maybe some pretzels.

MARSHA.   Fine. I'll be right back. *(Exits to kitchen area.)*

WANDA.   Oh, Jim-bo, she's a jewel. An absolute jewel. *(Wanda sits next to Jim.)*

JIM.   Thank you. We've been married 13 years.

WANDA.   Oh. An unlucky number. But she's a jewel. I hope she's not hard like a jewel — just precious.

JIM.   Yes, she's very precious.

WANDA.   Good.

JIM.   You know, I hate to say this, but I don't recognize your face actually.

WANDA.   That's very perceptive, Jim. I've had plastic surgery. But it wasn't the fancy-schmancy kind to make your face look better, it was so they couldn't find me.

JIM.   Who couldn't find you?

WANDA.   I don't want to talk about it. Not on the first night, at least.

JIM.   Now you've piqued my interest.

WANDA.   Oh, you men are always so impatient. *(Wanda squeezes his knee. Marsha comes in with the paté, and notices the knee-squeezing. Marsha sits down with the paté. Wanda is seated between Jim and Marsha.)*

MARSHA.   Here is the paté.

WANDA.   Thanks, honey, I'll just have the crackers. *(Munches enthusiastically on a cracker.)* Stoned wheat thins, I love this. *(To Jim.)* She's a jewel, Jim.

JIM.   *(Rather miserably.)* I know. You're a jewel, Marsha.

MARSHA.   Thank you. *(To Wanda.)* Would you like a drink? *(Wanda pauses for a moment, and then begins to sob, very genuinely. At a loss what to say.)* Don't feel you have to have a drink.

JIM.   Wanda, what's the matter?

WANDA.   *(Through sobs.)* Oh, I don't want to burden you. Or your wife.

MARSHA.   That's alright, I'm sure we'd love to be burdened.

I mean, if it would help you.

JIM. Yes. Tell us what's the matter.

WANDA. I don't know where to begin. I'm just so unhappy!

JIM. Gosh, Wanda. What is it? *(Wanda pulls herself together, and tries to explain why she felt so upset.)*

WANDA. Well it all started the summer after high school graduation. *(To Marsha.)* Jim and I had gone to the prom together, and though of course nothing had been said, everyone just kind of presumed he and I would get married.

JIM. Really? Who presumed this?

WANDA. Well, everyone. My mother, my father, me, everyone.

JIM. Gosh. I mean, I knew we dated.

WANDA. Dated, Jim-bo, we were inseparable. From about February of senior year to June senior year, we spent every spare moment together. You gave me your class ring. Look, I have it right here. *(Looks through her purse.)* No, I can't find it. *(Keeps looking.)*

MARSHA. Jim, gave me the nicest engagement ring.

WANDA. Uh, huh. Now, where is it? *(Wanda dumps out the messy contents of her purse; looks through the mess.)* No. No. Here's the prescription for Seconal I always carry with me in case I feel suicidal.

MARSHA. I don't think any of the pharmacies are open this late. *(Wanda stares at Marsha for a moment, like a child who's crying and has suddenly been distracted. Before she can go any further comprehending whatever Marsha said, Jim speaks up.)*

JIM. Forget about the ring, Wanda. Tell us why you cried a few minutes ago.

WANDA. Isn't it obvious?

JIM. Isn't what obvious?

WANDA. Seeing the path not taken. I could have had a happy life if I married you. Excuse me for talking this way, Marsha, I just want you to know how lucky you are.

MARSHA. Oh, that's fine. Whatever.

WANDA. No, not whatever. Jim-bo. *(Kisses him; looks at Marsha, speaks to Jim.)* You see, I do that in front of Marsha so she knows how lucky she is.

MARSHA.   Thank you. I feel lucky.

WANDA.   Well, don't you forget it. Are you listening to me?

MARSHA.   No one else is speaking.

WANDA.   *(Genuinely laughs.)* Oh I love her sense of humor. So anyway, after the prom, Jim-bo went away for the whole summer, and he didn't write me ...

JIM.   I didn't know you wanted me to ...

WANDA.   And then you and I went to different colleges, and *then* when you didn't write me, I was heartbroken ...

JIM.   Really? I'm terribly sorry ... I thought we were kind of casual. I mean, we were 17.

WANDA.   I was 18. They held me back in third grade.

JIM.   Wanda, if you felt this way, why didn't you tell me at the time? You haven't said anything in 20 years.

WANDA.   Well, I've been very busy, and it's hard to be open about emotions, especially painful ones. *(Chomps on a cracker.)* So then I went to Ann Arbor, and oh, Jim and Marsha, I'm so ashamed to tell you this — I was promiscuous.

MARSHA.   Really?

WANDA.   Yes. *(Emphatic, cranky.)* Gosh, these crackers are sure making me thirsty. When you offered me something to drink, I didn't think it was going to be my one chance.

MARSHA.   *(Startled, disoriented.)* I'm sorry. Would you like something to drink?

WANDA.   *(Sweetly.)* Yes, thank you, Marsha. Anything at all. Preferably with vodka. *(Marsha exits off to kitchen.)* She really is a jewel. She really is. Now where was I?

JIM.   You were saying you had been promiscuous.

WANDA.   It was awful. I became a campus joke. But it was because I was drowning my sorrow, you see — in flesh.

JIM.   In flesh. Ah. Well, that's too bad.

WANDA.   There was this one night a whole bunch of guys from the football team stood outside my window and they chanted my name.

JIM.   Oh. Well, at least you made an impression.

WANDA.   Yeah, but it was because I was missing a certain somebody. And also I liked sex. *(Marsha comes in, just in time to hear this last remark.)*

69

JIM. *(Startled.)* Oh, Marsha's here. Hello, Marsha. We missed you.

MARSHA. *(A bit of an edge.)* Here's your drink. I hope you like Kool-Aid.

WANDA. Oh, I love it! *(Gulps her entire drink.)* Mmmm, delicious. *(Marsha looks disappointed.)* So anyway, the campus minister once had to give a whole sermon against me, which made me feel just awful. *(To Jim.)* And all because I was pining for you.

MARSHA. I wonder if I should check on the chicken.

JIM. Please don't go just now. *(Jim gets up, to stand by Marsha.)*

WANDA. And, of course, I was raised Catholic, so I knew what I was doing was very very wrong, but I was so unhappy ... *(Weeps copiously. Jim and Marsha stare at her for a little while.)*

JIM. *(Without too much enthusiasm.)* There, there, Wanda.

MARSHA. Yes. There, there.

WANDA. And then my second husband gave me herpes, and every time the first one would call to threaten my life, it would trigger an outbreak.... *(Marsha sits back down in a chair, Jim sits on the arm.)* ... herpes is often set off by emotional turmoil, you know.

JIM. *(Forcing interest.)* Oh, yes, I've read that.

WANDA. And then I thought to hell with men, maybe I should become a lesbian. And I tried that, but the problem was I just wasn't attracted to women, so the whole experiment was a dismal failure.

MARSHA. Doesn't anyone want dinner yet?

WANDA. *(Suddenly switching moods.)* Marsha sounds hungry. Sure, honey, let's go eat. *(Wanda bounds up and moves to the dining room table. Jim and Marsha follow. The dinner is not realistically done. It may be mimed with plates and silverware already set on the table.)* Oh the dinner looks beautiful. Marsha, you're so talented as a homemaker. Now where was I?

JIM. Something about you were promiscuous.

WANDA. Well, I don't like to use that word. I slept around uncontrollably, that's what I prefer to say. Did you ever do that, Marsha?

MARSHA. No, I didn't. I was a late bloomer.

WANDA.   Uh huh. So then, there was that guy from prison. And then there was his father Fred. Did I tell you about Fred? Well, Fred said to me, I married you because I thought you would be my anchor in the port of life, but now I think you're stark raving mad ...

MARSHA.   Could I have the salt please? *(Jim passes Marsha the salt.)*

WANDA.   ... and I said, you think I'm crazy, who's the one who has hallucinations, and thinks that shoes go on the hands instead of the feet? Not me, buddy boy.

JIM.   *(To Wanda.)* Did he take drugs or something?

MARSHA.   Please don't ask her questions.

WANDA.   What?

MARSHA.   *(To Wanda.)* Well, I mean I want you to tell the story your own way.

WANDA.   Thank you, Marsha. You know, Jim, I really feel close to Marsha.

JIM.   I'm glad. *(To Marsha.)* Could I have the salt please?

WANDA.   *(Responding to him.)* Sure, honey. *(Passes him the salt; to Marsha.)* Don't you just love him? *(Continues on with story.)* So one day the washing machine blew up, and Fred said to me, you did that, everything about you is chaos, I'm leaving and I'm taking Tranquillity with me.

JIM.   He actually said "tranquillity"?

MARSHA.   *(Muttered.)* Don't ask her questions.

WANDA.   *(Explaining.)* Tranquillity was our dog. And I said, I'm the one who fed Tranquillity, and walked her and took care of her worms, and she used to throw up on the rug, and, of course, you can't just leave it there ...

MARSHA.   Excuse me, I'll be right back.

JIM.   Marsha, are you alright?

MARSHA.   I'm fine.

WANDA.   I hope my talking about vomit didn't make you feel sick.

MARSHA.   *(Nearly out of the room.)* No, it's fine. *(Marsha has left the dining area and gotten to the bathroom area. She holds her head in pain, or leans on a wall for a support. She just couldn't stand to be at the table for a minute longer.)*

71

WANDA.   She's a little hard to talk to.

JIM.   I think she had a hard day.

WANDA.   Really? What did she do? Spend it making up the guest room for me?

JIM.   Oh.

WANDA.   Really, I can sleep anywhere. I think I'm being evicted tomorrow anyway, so I'd prefer not to be there.

JIM.   That's too bad.

WANDA.   I roll with the punches. I enjoy the little things in life. I enjoy colors. I like textures, I like silk and cotton, I don't like corduroy, I don't like ridges ...

JIM.   *(On his way to find Marsha.)* Uh huh. Hold onto the thought. I'll be right back. *(Jim exits and goes to the bathroom area where he finds Marsha still crouched or leaning.)* Why are you hiding in the bathroom?

MARSHA.   I needed aspirin. Then I just couldn't go downstairs again. When is she leaving?

JIM.   I think she's staying overnight.

MARSHA.   What?

JIM.   I think she's staying ov ...

MARSHA.   Did she say that, or did you say that? *(Wanda, bored alone, bounds into the bathroom area with them. The area is small, and they're all crowded together.)*

WANDA.   What are you two talking about?

JIM.   Oh, nothing. Marsha was just brushing her teeth.

WANDA.   It's so intimate brushing your teeth, isn't it? When you live with someone, you don't have any secrets. I remember David said to me, why didn't you tell me you had herpes, and I said, I forgot, okay? People forget things, alright? And he said, not alright, I'm going to have this for life, and I said, so what, you have your nose for life, is that *my* fault?

MARSHA.   *(Tired, but sort of annoyed by the logic.)* Yes, but his nose wasn't your fault, while ...

WANDA.   What?

MARSHA.   Nothing. I see your point.

WANDA.   So then I thought I'd stay out of relationships for a while, and I went to work for this lawyer, only he wasn't a regular lawyer, he was a king pin.

JIM. King pin?

WANDA. Of crime. He was a king pin of crime, only I didn't realize it. Eventually, of course, I had to get my face re-done so they couldn't find me. But, I better not say anything more about this right now.

MARSHA. *(Trying to tell her no.)* Jim says you were expecting to stay over night ...

WANDA. Thank you, I'd love to! I feel I'm just starting to scratch the surface with old Jim-bo here. Jim-bo, do you remember that girl with the teeth who won Homecoming Queen, what was her name?

JIM. I don't remember. She had teeth?

WANDA. Big teeth.

MARSHA. I would like to leave the bathroom now.

WANDA. What?

MARSHA. Well, we need to make your room up for you. I didn't know you were ... well, we need to make it up ....

WANDA. *(A little girl.)* I hope there's a quilt. I love quilts.

MARSHA. I'll look for one. *(Wanda stares at her, happy, but doesn't get out of the way.)* You have to move or I can't get out of the bathroom.

WANDA. *(Serious.)* I'm holding you hostage.

MARSHA. What?

WANDA. *(Shifting, cheerful.)* Isn't it awful the way they take hostages now? *(Cheerfully leaves the bathroom, talking away.)* It reminds me of my life with Augie. He was really violent, but he was really little, so I was able to push him down the stairs. *(Jim and Marsha look at one another, a little alarmed by the "hostage" exchange. Lights change. The prominent sound of a clock ticking. Time is passing. Wanda, Jim and Marsha standing, in a "hallway" area, about to make their goodnights. Happy.)* Oh, you guys, it's been a great evening. I can't believe we played games for 4 hours!

MARSHA. I'm really sorry I shouted at you during Monopoly.

WANDA. That's okay. I know somebody who got killed playing Monopoly.

JIM. But you were really good at charades.

WANDA. Thanks, but I'm sorry I broke the lamp.

MARSHA.   It's perfectly alright. Now the guest room is right down this hall.

WANDA.   Well, good night, you two. See you in the morning.

MARSHA.   Good night. *(Wanda exits off to the guest room. Jim and Marsha go to their bedroom, or rearrange the set to stand in for a bedroom — move two chairs together into a "bed," put a comforter over themselves. They're too tired to talk. They kiss one another briefly, and close their eyes to sleep. Wanda enters, wrapped up in a quilt.)*

WANDA.   Oh, is this your bedroom? Oh, it's so pretty. *(Jim and Marsha open their eyes, very startled.)*

MARSHA.   Is something wrong with your room?

WANDA.   No, it's lovely. Although not as nice as here. But then this is the master bedroom, isn't it?

MARSHA.   Can I get you a pill?

WANDA.   No, thanks. Marsha, I love this bedroom. I feel very "enveloped" here. It makes me never want to leave. *(Wanda pulls up a chair right next to their bed. Keeps wrapped in her quilt.)* I just love New England. I worked in Hartford for three weeks once as a receptionist in a sperm bank.

MARSHA.   Wanda, I'm sorry. I really think I need to sleep.

WANDA.   You can sleep, I won't be offended. So I got fired from the sperm bank, and then I went to Santa Fe, 'cause I heard the furniture was nice there. *(Clock ticks. Time passes. Jim and Marsha change positions in bed.)* And then Arthur's ex-wife kept making threatening phone calls to me. *(Clock ticks. Jim and Marsha change positions, now look more uncomfortable. Coquettish.)* And I said, "Billy, why didn't you tell me you were 16?" *(Clock ticks. Chatty voice, just telling the facts.)* And then the policeman said, let me see your pussy, and I thought, hey, maybe this way I won't get a ticket. *(Clock ticks. Teary voice, telling a tragic turning point.)* And Leonard said, Wanda, you are a worthless piece of trash. And I said, don't you think I know that? Do you think this is news? *(Clock ticks. Energized, telling a fascinating story.)* And Howard said he wanted me to kill his mother, and I said, "Are you crazy? I've never even *met* your mother." And he said, "Alright, I'll introduce you." *(Jim and Marsha have closed their eyes, either asleep or pretending to be. Wanda looks over*

74

at them, suspicious.) Are you asleep? Jim? Marsha? *(Wanda looks to see if they're asleep. She shakes their shoulders a bit, to see if she can wake them.)* Jim? Marsha? You're not pretending to be asleep, are you? Jim? Marsha? *(Wanda opens Marsha's eyelid with her finger.)*

MARSHA.   Yes?

WANDA.   I was just checking if you were asleep.

MARSHA.   Yes I am. Goodnight. Sleep well.

WANDA.   Goodnight. *(Wanda takes her comforter and curls up at the bottom of their bed. Then she pulls their blanket off them, and on to her. Jim doesn't notice, he's asleep for real. Marsha is startled. But gives up, what to do. Lights dim. Clock ticks. Lights up for the morning. Wanda sound asleep. Jim and Marsha wake up, and abruptly leave the bedroom for the dining room area.)*

MARSHA.   You know, she doesn't snore. I'm really surprised.

JIM.   Want some coffee?

MARSHA.   I think I'd like some heroin.

JIM.   Maybe Wanda has some connections.

MARSHA.   I'm sure she does. Oh God, why did she sleep on our bed? She seemed like some insane nightmare Golden Retriever.

JIM.   Now I feel sorry for her.

MARSHA.   Well good for you. Was she always this way?

JIM.   Well she was always vivacious.

MARSHA.   I see. High school prom queen. Girl Most Likely to Get Herpes.

JIM.   Lots of people get herpes.

MARSHA.   Yes, but they don't talk about it for 3 hours.

JIM.   Why are you so hostile to her? *(Not meaning to say this.)* Is it because she's attracted to me?

MARSHA.   *(Not expecting to hear that.)* Yes. *(Marsha goes off to the kitchen.)*

JIM.   Are you getting coffee? *(Marsha re-enters with two coffee mugs, one of which she kind of shoves at Jim.)*

MARSHA.   And are you attracted to her?

JIM.   Now come on, Marsha, she's an emotional mess.

MARSHA.   You're putting up with it very patiently. Why is that?

JIM.   Well that's because ... I feel sympathy for her. She's someone I knew once who had a life, and look what's happened to her.

MARSHA.   She's attracted to you.

JIM.   Now don't make a big thing out of it. It's just slightly interesting for me, that's all.

MARSHA.   Well, fine. I understand. I think I'll make a trip to the nearest loony bin, and find some mental patient who finds *me* attractive. Then I'll bring him home and make you suffer through a 48 hour visit while he drools on the carpet.

JIM.   Oh, come on, stop making such a big deal about all this. It's no big deal ... it's just ... well, haven't you ever found it kind of exciting if someone finds you attractive?

MARSHA.   I've forgotten. *(Starts to leave.)* I'm going to the A & P. I have to get out of here. *(Marsha grabs a purse and exits.)*

JIM.   Don't be mad. *(Jim sighs. With his coffee he walks after her, but Wanda, stirring on the bed, hears him.)*

WANDA.   Is that life out there?

JIM.   You awake? *(Jim comes back into the bedroom area, holding his coffee mug.)*

WANDA.   Do I smell coffee? Oh, thanks, Jim-bo. *(Wanda takes Jim's coffee, thinking it's for her.)* Uh, I love this. You're like a little house slave. I knew I should've married you. Where's Marsha? Did she wake up dead or anything?

JIM.   No, she went to the A & P.

WANDA.   That's terrible of me to say. I don't want her dead. I'm just teasing 'cause I'm jealous of what she has.

JIM.   Oh, I'm not so special.

WANDA.   Oh, Jim-bo, you are. *(Wanda starts to get up; then shows a grimace of pain. A bit flirtatious.)* Uh. I've slept wrong on my back, I think. You know, a tense muscle or something.

JIM.   *(Thinking to himself, is this code?)* Oh. Your back is sore? Um, I'm not a professional masseur, but do you want me to rub it?

WANDA.   Oh, would you? *(Wanda pretty much flops over in delight. Jim starts to massage her back, sort of in the center.)* It's the lower back, Jim-bo.

JIM.   Oh. Okay. *(He starts to massage her lower back.)*
WANDA.   Uh. Yes. Oh yes. Oh, yes. Ohhhhhhh. Uhhhhhhhh.
(Marsha comes back in the house, holding the purse and car keys.
She stops and hears Wanda's moaning. She marches into the bedroom,
finds Jim and Wanda in the midst of their orgasmic back rub.)
MARSHA.   I'm back again, if anybody cares.
JIM.   *(Really jumps.)* Oh, Marsha. I didn't hear the car.
MARSHA.   I don't blame you. It was very noisy here.
JIM.   I'm ... giving Wanda ... that is, her back hurts.
WANDA.   He gives the most wonderful back-rub.
MARSHA.   I'm so pleased to hear it. Do you need the num-
ber of a back specialist, perhaps? I could call my doctor. If
you can't walk, we can arrange for an ambulance to take you
there.
JIM.   Now, Marsha, please, it's really quite innocent.
WANDA.   Hey, Marsha, really — I know he's your guy. *(To*
Jim.) You're her guy, Jim-bo. *(To Marsha.)* It's just my back
hurt.
MARSHA.   Yes, I follow what you say. Probably tension in the
lower back. I have a tension headache in the back of my head
today, it feels like it might split open. I think I'll go lie down.
In the guest room that you never got to. *(Starts to leave.)* Jim-
bo, when you finish with her back, the car has a flat tire on
the corner of Pleasantview and Maple. I thought you might
do something about that.
JIM.   Oh. I'll go now.
MARSHA.   No, finish the back-rub. You've convinced me it's
innocent, so finish it. *(Marsha walks out. Jim and Wanda look at*
one another uncomfortably.)
WANDA.   Well, she said to finish it.
JIM.   I don't feel comfortable with her in the house.
WANDA.   Look, she said it was fine, let's take her at her
word. *(Jim looks dubious and touches her back lightly. At the merest*
touch, Wanda starts to moan loudly again.)
JIM.   *(Stopping the back-rub.)* Can't you be more quiet?
WANDA.   It feels so good.
JIM.   Look, that's enough. I'm gonna go deal with the flat
tire.

WANDA.   Can I come?

JIM.   Why don't you … soak in the bathtub for your back?

WANDA.   Alright. Thank you for the back-rub, Jim-bo. *(Gets up; calls after where Marsha went.)* Marsha? Do you have any bubble bath? *(Marsha comes back.)*

MARSHA.   What?

WANDA.   Do you have any bubble bath? Jim won't continue with the back rub, and I need to relax.

MARSHA.   *(Thrown by re-mention of the backrub.)* The back rub … I … what was the question?

JIM.   Bubble bath. Do we have some?

MARSHA.   Yes, I'm sure we do. Maybe Jim would like to pour it on you in the bathtub.

JIM.   Marsha. Please.

WANDA.   Oooh, kinky. *(Loudly.)* Hey! I have an idea! Why don't I cook dinner for you guys tonight? Do you like octopus?

MARSHA.   Thank you, Wanda, no. I thought we'd go to a restaurant tonight. The walls in this house are starting to vibrate.

WANDA.   They are?

MARSHA.   Yes. So we'll go to a nice, soothing restaurant where they will take care of us. Alright?

WANDA.   Sure! Fine by me. *(Lights change. Maybe lovely classical music to change the mood. Jim, Marsha, Wanda sit at the table. The Waiter comes out and puts a tasteful flower arrangement on the table, turning it into the restaurant.)* This is such a pretty restaurant. The music is so classical.

WAITER.   Enjoy your meal.

JIM.   Thank you. *(Waiter exits. Wanda and Jim mime eating from their plates.)*

WANDA.   Ohhh, I think I know someone. *(Waves, calls out to imaginary table.)* Hi, there! *(To Jim and Marsha.)* Oh, no, I don't know them. *(Calls out again.)* Never mind! I thought you were my gynecologist.

MARSHA.   You thought he'd be up here?

WANDA.   Well, he travels a lot. He also sells encyclopedias. *(Waiter re-enters with a tray of wine glasses. He gives each person a wine glass, Wanda last.)*

WAITER.   And here is your wine.

WANDA.   They didn't have Kool-Aid?

WAITER.   White Zinfandel was the closest we could get, Madam.

WANDA.   Well, alright. *(To Marsha and Jim.)* Here's mud in your eye. *(Everyone drinks. All of them finish their drinks in several quick gulps. The Waiter starts to leave.)*

JIM.   Waiter! *(Makes signal to Waiter of "another round." The Waiter nods and exits.)*

WANDA.   I can't believe they didn't have octopus. It's a delicacy.

JIM.   *(Referring to their plates.)* Well, the trout's pretty good.

WANDA.   Yeah, but they put nuts on it or something.

JIM.   Well, eat around them maybe.

WANDA.   You know, Jim, tomorrow we should get out the old yearbook. You know, Marsha, you wouldn't believe how dashing he was back then. *(To Jim.)* Not that you're not now, of course.

JIM.   You're sure a shot for my ego.

MARSHA.   I'd like to shoot your ego.

JIM.   What?

MARSHA.   Nothing. Go back to talking about high school. I'll try to achieve a Zen state. *(Closes her eyes, puts her arms loose by her side, tries to relax her body.)*

JIM.   I ... I wonder where the waiter is with the drinks.

MARSHA.   *(With eyes closed; chant-like.)* I am sitting by a tree, and there's a lovely breeze.

WANDA.   This restaurant is so adorable. This whole town. You know what I'm thinking? I'm thinking of maybe moving up here to the country with you all, finding a little house to rent. Nothing's happening in my life right now, this might be just the change I might need. *(The Waiter arrives with three more glasses of wine, which he passes out to them. Marsha's eyes are open again; Wanda's comments above pretty much blew her attempt at a Zen state.)* I'm almost through with my facial surgery. I've had everything done on my face except my nose. I kept that the same.

79

JIM. You're right. I recognize your nose now. Yes.

WAITER. Will there be anything else?

WANDA. What? Done to my face?

WAITER. Anything else I can do for you at the restaurant?

JIM. We wanted three more glasses of wine.

WAITER. I just brought them.

JIM. Oh. So you did. Well, thank you. *(The Waiter leaves. Wanda starts to eat her fish.)*

MARSHA. So you're going to move up here, are you? Going to sweep up and stick your feet in the ground and root yourself in our "little neck of the woods," are you?

JIM. Marsha, we don't own this area.

MARSHA. I feel differently. *(To Wanda.)* I don't want you moving here, is that clear? I don't want you invading my life with your endless ravings anymore, is that clear? *(The Waiter returns. Wanda keeps eating, seemingly just listening to what's being said, finding it interesting rather than upsetting.)*

WAITER. Is everything alright?

MARSHA. No, everything is not alright, this woman is trying to invade my life, and this man is too stupid to see it, and hide from her. *(To Jim.)* Don't you realize she's insane?

JIM. Marsha, could we just finish dinner please?

MARSHA. No, I'd like the check.

WAITER. Are you unhappy with your fish?

MARSHA. I'm very unhappy with it. It has too many bones in it. *(Almost on cue, Wanda starts choking on a bone. She gasps and chokes. Jim, Marsha and the Waiter look at her shocked for a moment.)*

JIM. Shouldn't one of us do the Heimlich maneuver?

MARSHA. I don't want to do it, I don't like her. *(Wanda looks startled, even in the midst of her choking. She keeps choking and pointing to her throat.)*

JIM. Marsha! *(To Waiter.)* Can you do it?

WAITER. I don't know how to do it yet. It's my first day. Can't you do it?

JIM. Oh, very well. *(Jim gets up and gets the choking Wanda to stand. He stands behind her and then, not sure what to do, puts his arms under her arms, and locks his hands behind her neck: that*

80

is, he puts her in a half-Nelson, and keeps jerking her head forward
with his hands, hopefully, as if this should fix her choking.)
MARSHA. *(After a second.)* Oh, for God's sake. *(Marsha gets*
up, pushes Jim away. She stands behind Wanda, puts her arms
around Wanda's lower stomach and then rather violently and sud-
denly pulls her arms into Wanda's lower stomach. This does the trick,
and Wanda spits out the bit of fish and bone, and starts to breathe
again. Wanda sits back down, exhausted.)
WANDA.   Oh, thank God, I thought I was a goner. *(Suddenly*
into the restaurant burst two men with handkerchiefs tied around their
mouths, and carrying guns. They aim their guns at everyone, but
make straight for Wanda.)
MAN.   There she is!
WANDA.   Oh my God, they've found me! *(The men grab her*
and, pointing the guns at everyone else, drag Wanda out of the restau-
rant. Being dragged or carried out:) Oh, God, it's the king pin.
Help me! Jim! Jim! *(All this happens very fast and very suddenly.*
And now Wanda is gone. Jim, Marsha and the Waiter seem stunned
for a moment. A "talking-to-the-audience" light comes up, and the Waiter
crosses down into it and addresses the audience.)
WAITER.   The next day at the restaurant was considerably
less intense, and eventually as time went on, I was made head
waiter. For a while I liked the added responsibility and the
additional money, but after a while, I realized I wasn't doing
what I wanted to do with my life. I wanted to be an actor.
But then the story isn't really about me. *(Humbly, the Waiter*
exits. Jim and Marsha look confused by the Waiter's behavior, and
now address the audience themselves again. They also straighten the
set a bit, while they talk, so that it resembles their house as it was at
the beginning of the play.)
JIM.   *(To audience.)* Well, all that happened a few weeks ago.
Wanda hasn't been found yet, but she's probably fine.
MARSHA.   I feel guilty about what happened. I wasn't a good
hostess.
JIM.   Now, honey, she's probably fine. Wanda's sort of like a
bacteria — wherever she is, she seems to grow and go on and
on just fine, so you shouldn't feel bad.
MARSHA.   Yes, but right before Wanda started to choke on

the fish bone, I had this momentary, stray thought of wishing she would choke on a fish bone. And then suddenly she did. I know it's not logical, but on some level, I feel I tried to kill her. And then thugs came and carried her away. I mean, in a way, it's just what I wanted.

JIM. Now, Marsha, you're not responsible for what happened.

MARSHA. I chose the restaurant.

JIM. Now, Marsha. You're not omnipotent. Besides, awful things are always happening to Wanda. She's like a magnet for trouble.

MARSHA. *(To the audience.)* Well, it was just the most awful two days. Three days, counting meeting with the police.

JIM. But some good came out of it.

MARSHA. Yes. We had a big argument, and that was good.

JIM. It cleared the air.

MARSHA. I said what I was feeling, and it was mostly negative, but it was good to say it.

JIM. It cleared the air.

MARSHA. And one of the things I said was that we don't feel joy enough. Or hardly at all.

JIM. Right. We don't feel joy much. So we joined an aerobics class ...

MARSHA. To get the blood moving.... When you move around, you tend to feel better ...

JIM. And we're going to a marriage counselor who specializes in breaking down fear of intimacy in people who've known one another for over 10 years ...

MARSHA. And, of course, we fit that. And all told, I guess Wanda's visit helped to stir us up in a good way, all told.

JIM. Right.

MARSHA. Blessings come in unexpected ways.

JIM. Right.

MARSHA. Now if only we were happy.

JIM. Right. *(They look at one another. Then they look out at the audience. Some friendly, possibly optimistic music plays. Lights dim on Jim and Marsha. End of play.)*

BUSINESS LUNCH
AT THE RUSSIAN
TEA ROOM

BUSINESS LUNCH AT THE RUSSIAN TEA ROOM was part of the six-play evening, DURANG/DURANG, produced at Manhattan Theatre Club (Lynne Meadow, Artistic Director; Barry Grove, Managing Director) in New York City on November 14, 1994. It was directed by Walter Bobbie; the set design was by Derek McLane; the costume design was by David C. Woolard; the lighting design was by Brian Nason; the sound design was by Tony Meola; the production stage manager was Perry Cline and the stage manager was Gregg Fletcher. The cast was as follows:

CHRIS, a playwright .... Keith Reddin
MARGARET, his agent .... Patricia Elliott
WAITER .... Marcus Giamatti
MELISSA STEARN .... Patricia Randell
PRIEST .... David Aaron Baker
RABBI .... Lizbeth Mackay

NOTE: At MTC we didn't list the Priest and Rabbi as characters; we didn't want the audience to expect to see them. So in production, I'd prefer you didn't list them as well.

Also, at MTC, we cast an actress as the Rabbi because all three actors already had parts in the play. Since Keith Reddin had been playing children and women for much of the evening up until now, it seemed only fitting, and kind of fun, to have Lizbeth Mackay play the male rabbi. However, if you are using a larger company and want to cast a male as the rabbi that is fine also.

BUSINESS LUNCH
AT THE RUSSIAN
TEA ROOM

Chris, a playwright, is going through a large basket of laundry, mostly white sweat socks. He is laboriously matching the socks, checking the tops of the socks to see if the stripes are blue or red or black, thin or thick, etc.

The phone rings.

On another part of the stage is Margaret, Chris' agent. She is holding a phone, calling him. She is any age over 45, worldly, smart, quick, a little inexact in her listening.

Chris answers the phone, which is near his laundry. (It can be a cordless battery phone.)

CHRIS.   Hello?

MARGARET.   Hello, Chris, it's me. Are you awake yet?

CHRIS.   Is this public television again? I *have* renewed my membership, and I don't care about the umbrella, so please stop calling.

MARGARET.   Chris, this is your agent.

CHRIS.   Oh, Margaret. Hi.

MARGARET.   Are you writing on your play?

CHRIS.   No. No, I'm doing laundry. I'm matching socks actually. Making sure I don't put a blue stripe with a black stripe, or a thin double red stripe with a thick single red stripe.

MARGARET.   Well, that won't earn me my 10%, will it?

CHRIS.   No. But I need socks in order to wear shoes.

MARGARET.   Yes, yes, details. Um ... I'm reminding you that you have a meeting at the Russian Tea Room with Melissa

Stearn.

CHRIS. Oh, right, yes, I'd almost forgotten. Who is she again?

MARGARET. She's a new script development person at Zovirax.

CHRIS. Zovirax? Isn't that a medication for cold sores?

MARGARET. Oh, is it? Well, maybe it's Zylaphone. You know, one of those film production companies. She's apparently very hot in Hollywood right now. And she likes writers from the theatre. Apparently Lanford Wilson wrote something for her.

CHRIS. Oh well, that's good. Do you have any checks coming in for me?

MARGARET. Well, the royalty for your one act is coming in.

CHRIS. How much is it again?

MARGARET. $250.

CHRIS. Oh yes. That's not very much.

MARGARET. Now, darling, the play was only 10 minutes.

CHRIS. It was half an hour.

MARGARET. Well, it just flew by. Chrissy, dear, we know theatre pays less, that's why you should go meet with Melba Stringer, and make one of those development deals. Write a movie, write a TV show.

CHRIS. Melba Stringer?

MARGARET. Who's Melba Stringer?

CHRIS. You mean, Melissa Stearn.

MARGARET. Yes, Melissa Stearn. Call me later. (*Hangs up and exits. The sound of chatter and clinking silverware. The stage transforms itself into the Russian Tea Room. The Russian Tea Room has a lot of red in it. A booth appears; the booth is in the form of a half-circle, and the seating and back are made of red leather or Naugahyde. A round table with a pink table cloth on top of it fits into the booth. This may be achieved with stage hands dressed as waiters. But however it's done, it should be fast and a little overwhelming. Chris does not exit, but lets this activity swirl around him. He is still holding his laundry basket. He sits in the booth that's been brought out, and puts his laundry basket on the seat next to him. A Waiter, in a red tunic with a Russian feel to it, brings him a bowl of something.*)

WAITER. Here's your borscht, sir.

CHRIS.   I didn't order borscht. This isn't mine.

WAITER.   *(A bit surly.)* You don't want it?

CHRIS.   I didn't order it. I just got here.

WAITER.   *(As if Chris had changed his mind.)* I'll take it back then. *(Exits. Enter Melissa Stearn. She's in her late 20s, early 30s. Very high energy, very forceful. Dressed in a "power" dress. 100% sure of her opinions, and loves the movie business.)*

MELISSA.   Christopher! Melissa Stearn. I'm sorry, I'm late, I just flew in from L.A. and the limousine got stuck in traffic, but luckily I ran into Kim Basinger in the airport, and she rode in the car with me, so I had a movie star to talk to the whole way. I'm so pleased to meet you. I love your work. *Prelude to a Kiss* was my favorite play, it was my life story exactly.

CHRIS.   It was your life story? You mean, on your wedding day your spirit left your body and entered the body of an old man?

MELISSA.   Well, not literally, of course, but I just loved the play. It was my life story exactly. Although I've never been married, I like to have affairs with black men, and then just move on from one to another. Eventually I'll have a baby though, I think that's part of the point of being a woman, you should do every thing once.

CHRIS.   Uh huh. You mean, ice hockey. Mass murder. Working in a library.

MELISSA.   Exactly. Waiter! *(She's so certain of herself that the Waiter comes immediately.)* I'll have blinis and beluga, and a tall ice tea, stirred with a stick not a spoon. And what will you have?

CHRIS.   I'll have scrambled eggs.

MELISSA.   You should have borscht. It's delicious here.

WAITER.   He doesn't like borscht.

CHRIS.   Thank you for remembering.

MELISSA.   Bring it to him anyway. *(Waiter starts to exit.)*

CHRIS.   I'll have scrambled eggs please. *(Waiter exits; we don't know if he heard Chris or not.)*

MELISSA.   Christopher, all of us at Zerofax feel that we want to return to the old-fashioned kind of movie where the characters have dialogue and thoughts and emotions — you know, like *Four Weddings and a Funeral*, we think that was great, you know, Hugh Grant and romance and people buying tickets. That's what it's about, and that's what makes Zerofax a different kind of movie company. We're interested in quality.

CHRIS.   You know. I have to tell you, I didn't actually write *Prelude to a Kiss*. That was Craig Lucas.

MELISSA.   Oh, that's right. Well, he wasn't available, so then we called you. My assistant Janet loves your work, she said, why don't you call Christopher, he's a very funny writer. And I thought that was a brilliant idea.

CHRIS.   Thank you.

MELISSA.   I love theatre writers. I produced *Sleaze-O-Rama* for television last year. Did you see it? It got great numbers. It was about a serial killer who became president but who found his humanity after he got Aids and died. Everyone loved it. Lanford Wilson wrote the first script, which was beautiful, but we had to throw it out because none of the network people liked it, so we had Babaloo Feldman rewrite every single word. But Lanford understood. He thought we wanted something sensitive, but we didn't. I hope he brings the caviar soon, I have a meeting with Nora Ephron in 15 minutes. Nora Ephron is the kind of quality writer we want to work with. That's why I'm meeting with you as well.

CHRIS.   Thank you.

MELISSA.   We want Nora to write a movie for Meg Ryan where Meg is a widow who misses her husband dreadfully, they had this really special relationship, and then some man hears her talking on the radio, and he's really moved by what she says and he wants to contact her, but the switch is it's her husband who hears her on the radio, she's not a widow at all, he disappeared at sea just like Julia Roberts did in that movie watcha-ma-call-it, and then he shows up and he kills her. It's sort of like *Sleepless in Seattle* meets *Psycho*. What was that Julia Roberts movie called?

CHRIS.   *Sleeping with the Enemy?*

MELISSA.   Yes. *Sleeping with the Enemy in Seattle.* Something like that. Waiter! I need my food *now* please. *(Waiter had just started to enter with food.)*

WAITER. Alright, alright, here's your fucking caviar. *(Gives her caviar, gives Chris borscht.)*

MELISSA. Oh, terrific. I love caviar. Not the taste exactly, but the sense of status it gives me. It's sort of like going to the bank and eating your money. Mmmmmm, delicious. Yummy.

CHRIS. *(To Waiter.)* I didn't order borscht. I don't like borscht. I want scrambled eggs. Truthfully I'd like a BLT, but I'm sure the Russian Tea Room doesn't have BLTs.

WAITER. Enjoy your meal. Fuck you. *(Exits.)*

CHRIS. Why is he being so rude?

MELISSA. Rudeness doesn't bother me. Stupidity does, but not rudeness. I love to stand in a long line, and then just walk to the front and cut in, and if someone doesn't like it, I just say: Fuck you! Oh, you ordered the borscht. Good for you. I thought you didn't like it. So do we have a deal? Do you want to write the movie?

CHRIS. What movie?

MELISSA. Oh I haven't told you the idea. I told you the Nora Ephron. *(Suddenly serious.)* Now that's meant for her. Don't steal it, we'll sue you. I'm involved in six lawsuits right now, one of them against my mother. I'm gonna make her beg. *(Back to energy, friendliness.)* Now here's the idea for you. Shall I tell you?

CHRIS. I guess so. I'm here.

MELISSA. Okay. Here goes. *(Carefully, so the excellence can be savored.)* It's about a Catholic priest and a rabbi, who fall in love and then, O. Henry-style, each has a sex change without telling the other one.

CHRIS. Ah.

MELISSA. So do you want to do it?

CHRIS. Um....

MELISSA. You see, you're the perfect person because Janet tells me you know all about the Catholic Church, you wrote a play about it once, you went to Catholic school apparently for 100 years or something ...

CHRIS. Yes, well, twelve years.

MELISSA. That's amazing. You must have incredible stories.

CHRIS. *(His energy seeping away.)* Uh huh.

MELISSA. And so this story is perfect for you.

CHRIS. *(Has trouble saying no.)* Well, I'm glad you thought of me, but ... you know ...

MELISSA. What? Don't you think it's brilliant?

CHRIS. Yes, but ... I don't really know anything about rabbis.

MELISSA. Well, we'll call up a Jew and get them to tell you. I had dinner once with Philip Roth, I'll call him at home. *(Takes out her mobile phone.)*

CHRIS. No, please, don't call him yet. I'm not sure if this idea is right for me.

MELISSA. It's a great idea. Conceptual, but with lots of feeling. I wonder if you can do feeling. Well, we'll get Bo Goldman to come in and put in some feeling. But we really think you'll understand the religious angle.

CHRIS. Uh huh.

MELISSA. Do you like the idea?

CHRIS. Uh, well, I can see why you want to do it.

MELISSA. This idea really pushes the envelope.

CHRIS. Yes it does.

MELISSA. So when can you start?

CHRIS. I'm not sure that I'm available actually. I'm trying to write a play, and I have some letters to answer. And I haven't finished sorting my laundry.

MELISSA. I think it's great you brought your laundry to the Russian Tea Room. Very individual. Janet said you were a real person. And I like that, because I'm a real person.

CHRIS. Funny. You don't seem like one.

MELISSA. That's just my LA cover. Underneath I'm a real person, with throbbing, shrieking needs and neuroses. If we work together, you'll get to see that side of me. My mother knows that side. She's gonna go bankrupt and then if she apologizes in public, maybe we'll keep her from going to jail.

CHRIS. Really. Now that sounds like an interesting story.

MELISSA. No, no, just mother-daughter stuff, you know, competition for the father, the mother's a bitch. It's been done. *Terms of Endearment, Postcards from the Edge.* It's not new, it's not fresh. Now this priest-rabbi-sex-change-but-it's-touching, that's new.

CHRIS.   Gee, I'm very flattered, but I don't think I actually want to do it. I can't explain why. Sometimes I make decisions intuitively.

MELISSA.   I'm not sensitive. You don't like this idea? I have 22 more of them. Wanna hear?

CHRIS.   Shouldn't you be getting to Nora Ephron?

MELISSA.   I have a helicopter waiting to take me to the upper west side, so I have a couple more minutes still. Let me tell you my other ideas.

CHRIS.   Alright.

MELISSA.   Did you see the movie *Cruising?*

CHRIS.   Yes.

MELISSA.   S & M murders. Al Pacino as an undercover cop posing as a homosexual in leather.

CHRIS.   Yes, I remember it.

MELISSA.   Re-do the whole movie, but with children.

CHRIS.   What? You mean 10 year olds in leather?

MELISSA.   Exactly. Did you see *Bugsy Malone?* It would be like that, only sick. We could get Gus Van Sant.

CHRIS.   Yes, I might write that one. Wouldn't we all go to prison?

MELISSA.   Clinton likes Hollywood. We'd get Janet Reno to give us a special dispensation.

CHRIS.   Uh huh. Well, I can't believe we'd be allowed to make that movie.

MELISSA.   Push the envelope. Back in 1939 they couldn't say "Frankly, my dear, I don't give a damn." Now we can say fuck and show decapitations. So life moves forward.

CHRIS.   *(Calls.)* Check please.

MELISSA.   No, no, I'll pick up the check, every word I say is tax deductible, 80%. Mmmm, this caviar is delicious. I don't want to gain weight though. Excuse me while I make myself throw up in the ladies room, and then I'll just hop in that helicopter and go see Nora Ephron. I'll call your agent, you tell me which idea you want to write, the priest-rabbi thing or the kiddie *Cruising.* Either one is fine, we just want quality but accessibility, something everyone in the world can iden-

91

tify with. It's going to be great. Zerofax is really excited about working with you. It was great meeting you. *(Melissa puts out her hand; before Chris takes it, she puts her fingers down her throat and starts to gag.)* Which way is the ladies room, do you know? *(Puts fingers down throat some more; exits. At Melissa's exit, the restaurant transforms itself away again. Chris gets out of the booth and grabs back his laundry basket, as the booth disappears away. We are now back in Chris's apartment, where he had been folding laundry before. Phone rings again. It's Margaret.)*

CHRIS.   Hello?

MARGARET.   Hello, Crissy. This is Margaret. How did your meeting with Melissa Stearn go?

CHRIS.   It went very well.

MARGARET.   Do you want to write it?

CHRIS.   I think I need to finish matching my socks, and then maybe take a bath. Then I need to take my brain out and let it soak overnight in Clorox or something, and then ... maybe I should consider moving to Europe.

MARGARET.   Oh you didn't like her. Well, just take a nap. She's not the only person in Hollywood.

CHRIS.   Yes, but sometimes it feels like she is.

MARGARET.   Now, now. Don't overreact. Sleep on it. Remove her personality from the equation, and maybe her idea is actually good. Trust me, open your mind, don't be so judgmental. Mull over the idea for the evening. Alright?

CHRIS.   Alright. *(Margaret and Chris both hang up. Margaret exits. Chris stares and tries to think through Melissa's idea.)* A priest. A rabbi. They fall in love. It's funny, it's touching. Different cultures, they clash, they contrast. Easter versus Passover. Baptism versus briss. They meet cute, in an S & M bar with Al Pacino. No, that's the other idea. They meet at a communion breakfast. *(Church bells are heard. On a different part of the stage, enter a handsome young Priest.)*

PRIEST.   *(Out, to imaginary person.)* Good morning, Mrs. McGillicutty. Thank you, I'm glad you liked the sermon.

CHRIS.   He's young, he's handsome, he's celibate. Rabbi Teitelbaum comes into the church, looking confused. *(Enter the Rabbi. He is dressed as an orthodox rabbi, and has a beard and a*

black hat.)
RABBI.   Oy, oy, vhere am I?
PRIEST.   May I help you?
CHRIS.   Their eyes meet. They consider dating. They go to discos. *(Suddenly disco music, flashing lights. The Priest and Rabbi start dancing together. From another part of the stage, Melissa appears ... a voice in Chris's head.)*
MELISSA.   No, no, no, not vulgar. We want sensitivity. Zerofax is big on sensitivity.
CHRIS.   They don't go to a disco. They go for long walks in the autumn. They discover one another's humanity. *(Sweet music. The Priest and Rabbi hold hands, mime walking.)*
RABBI.   Vhat beautiful trees. I see God's face in the autumn leaves.
PRIEST.   Yes, Rabbi, me, too.
RABBI.   Oy, oy, but I feel so guilty.
PRIEST.   Don't feel guilty. Oh, Moishe. Even though we have different beliefs, I see more and more that your immortal soul looks just like mine.
MELISSA.   Yeah, but sexy. Sensitive, but sexy. *(The Priest and Rabbi stop walking, look at one another intently.)*
PRIEST.   You make me hot.
RABBI.   You make me hot too.
PRIEST.   I don't think I'm gay, and yet I long to touch your penis.
RABBI.   Oy, oy, please, I'm a rabbi.
PRIEST.   It's a sin. But can love be a sin?
RABBI.   I think it can.
MELISSA.   Good. Good tension. Sex versus religious belief. Excellent. They're gay, they're not gay. Makes it easier to cast the actors. *Philadelphia* made money, but they didn't kiss enough. Have them kiss.
PRIEST.   I feel so drawn to you, Moishe.
RABBI.   Oh, Patrick, Patty boy, even though it's against the Torah, inside my heart I know I want to schtupp you.
PRIEST.   Oh, Moishe. Oh yes, oh yes. *(The Priest and Rabbi keep looking intently at one another.)*
MELISSA.   We don't need them to say "schtupping," that's

bad writing. Just have them kiss, and we'll cut to a close-up of their tongues. *(The Priest and Rabbi embrace and kiss intensely.)*

CHRIS.   Then there's an earthquake, and God strikes them dead. It's a replay of Sodom and Gomorrha, and He kills the priest and the rabbi ... *(Aimed at Melissa.)* ... and everyone in the movie business in Los Angeles.

MELISSA.   Good idea, but save it for the end. They haven't had their sex changes yet.

CHRIS.   I don't want to write this. *(The Priest and Rabbi have been continuing to kiss, but at the above line, they stop and look at Chris.)*

MELISSA.   Keep kissing. *(The Priest and Rabbi go back to kissing.)* No, keep writing, you're doing well.

CHRIS.   No, I won't write this. It's idiotic. You should write it yourself, you like the idea so much. *(The Priest and Rabbi stop kissing again when Chris says "I won't write this." They stare at Chris and Melissa.)*

MELISSA.   Good idea! I'll write it myself. I'll get help from Nora and Bo and Babaloo. I'll pay myself $300,000. It'll be great! *(She exits, happy.)*

CHRIS.   *(To himself.)* So I don't make the money. So what. I'm going to focus on what's simple and true. I'm going to fold my laundry. *(With dignity and importance, he starts to match his socks. The Priest and the Rabbi come over to Chris.)*

PRIEST.   May we help?

CHRIS.   Please. *(The Priest and Rabbi help match the socks.)* Red stripe with red stripe. Double blue stripe with double blue stripe. Light blue stripe with light blue stripe. Green sock with green sock. *(Chris, Rabbi and Priest keep trying to match the socks. For some reason it is very hard to make a match. The Rabbi in particular keeps holding up one sock with another, and discovering that it is not a match. They are not upset or frustrated doing this. It's just the task they've committed to do. Happy, contended music plays. Lights fade on Chris, the Priest and the Rabbi, matching the socks from the laundry basket.)*

NOTES ON PERFORMING
AND PRODUCING DURANG/DURANG

My plays seem to be tricky to perform. I have found that whether a play of mine comes across as funny or funny-touching or loud-and-off-putting or overstated-and-false varies wildly from production to production, depending on the acting tone that is found.

I don't believe there is only one way to perform a play — but really, you don't look at Blanche DuBois in A STREETCAR NAMED DESIRE and say: "I think I'm going to play her like a lascivious loudmouth." And then walk around the stage bellowing and belching while you say "Young, young, young man."

I suppose that seems outlandish as a suggestion, but I have seen the tone and effectiveness of my plays change totally depending on how they're done. And my plays often are written in an exaggerated style that actors and directors sometimes mistakenly think they must match. Finding the truthful psychological underpinnings to the characters in my plays is *very* important.

So, for those reasons, I write these notes, geared to guiding actors and directors to find the right tone.

And some readers of plays have told me they enjoy the notes. So I hope you do too. And if not, sorry.

So on to specifics.

MRS. SORKEN

About The Play

In the late eighties, I had an evening called MRS. SORKEN
PRESENTS at the American Repertory Theatre in Cambridge,
Massachusetts, with Elizabeth Franz playing Mrs. Sorken. For
that evening, I wrote three appearances for her, before each
of three plays she was introducing. And the character's first
appearance always went very well, but the subsequent ones
kind of did not. It felt as if the audience was unwilling to re-
enter Mrs. Sorken's contemplative, verbal world after they had
been involved with specific plays.

So I put the speech away, though I hoped I'd find a future
use for the character, since I liked her. Then when Manhattan Theatre Club expressed interest in doing an evening of
one acts by me, I resurrected the character, rewrote some of
what she says, and decided to limit her appearance to just at
the beginning of the evening.

About Acting The Character

Mrs. Sorken is happy to talk to the audience, and she has no
trouble expressing herself. Thus stage fright, or upset at mis-
placing her notes, is not meant to be part of her character.

Although it's logical to play momentary disorientation, I want
her to quickly move on. I want her to play that she's immediately resilient, that she has most of what she needs to say in
her head, and that she believes other ideas will pop into her
head whenever she needs them to; and then I want her to just
get on with the task of communicating the words and content
of the speech.

Mrs. Sorken is very verbal, her speech is dense. So please do not speak slowly.

Or as director Walter Bobbie would say to the all actors in DURANG/DURANG: aim for the end of the sentence, don't break it up into little pieces.

Another piece of director advice: act *on* the lines, not between them.

If you've been acting on the line, and not pausing in between, when later you *choose* to take a pause, it can be very powerful, because you've "earned" the pause. But you can only earn one from time to time; not every other sentence.

Walter often told the actors to pay attention to the commas and the periods in my writing, especially in long speeches. And to predominantly follow them. Thus the opening sentence is: "Dear theatergoers, welcome, and how lovely to see you." I don't mean for you to abnormally rush it, but the pauses should be very tiny, as a comma suggests; and not a full stop, as a period would suggest. Because if you choose to stop after the word "theatergoers" and then stop after "welcome," you make the first sentence somewhat laborious. You take one thought, and make it into three thoughts. And if you should do that throughout the speech, the audience will feel bogged down and tired of all of Mrs. Sorken's words.

I honestly don't mean to be a controlling ogre. Sure ... if you have an acting impulse to stop at a certain place or to stress a certain word, that's fine.

But as a general rule, go for the end of the sentence, always be communicating the *whole* sentence — it helps the audience understand what you're saying. And with Mrs. Sorken's complicated and formal diction, it's good to help them hear the whole thought, all at once, not broken up into separate little beats.

If you go too slowly, the audience will get ahead of you.

Plus with Mrs. Sorken or Amanda in BELLE or the woman in LAUGHING WILD or Sister Mary — any of the characters I've written who talk in long, convoluted sentences — you must perform them with a high energy, you mustn't dawdle through them. Pace, pace, verbal dexterity. Look at the screwball comedies of the 1930s, and watch how fast everybody talks (*Bringing Up Baby* with Katharine Hepburn and Cary Grant, *The Lady Eve* with Barbara Stanwyck and Henry Fonda, *His Girl Friday* with Rosalind Russell and Cary Grant). Pray to cinematic heaven, and ask it to guide you.

Two additional things about Mrs. Sorken:

Sometimes the humor can lie in saying something matter-of-factly — as when she says "Maybe after he dies I'll go somewhere," or when she identifies with the "poor Mormon woman in ANGELS IN AMERICA."

And also, don't be afraid to figure out what words Mrs. Sorken enjoys saying. Mrs. Sorken's language is ornate, she uses words and phrases like "etymology" and "sedating tablet" and "teeming unconscious." So when your instincts lead you to it, relish the fancy words. It's hard to say "teeming unconscious" without enjoying the word "teeming" a little bit. "Photosynthesis" is probably slightly pleasurable to say.

I don't intend for Mrs. Sorkin to be British, but I must admit many of my inspirations for this kind of humor are British. All those wonderful, scatter-brained ladies in British movie comedies, like Margaret Rutherford or Joyce Grenfell. Very polite, very optimistic, willing to put a chipper spin on whatever they do.

But I do prefer that you not use a British accent, or for that matter a "Connecticut" lockjaw one. Just use your own voice, and let the character sound how you sound, saying and believing what Mrs. Sorken says.

I don't mean to inhibit your acting impulses. But if you had experienced the difference between, say, Patricia Elliott at Manhattan Theatre Club doing the speech in a charming, funny way that took ten minutes and, say, another actress taking many pauses and making the piece be close to twenty minutes — I think you would understand my desire to guide actors through these notes.

Well, that's all. When in doubt, have fun.

Alternative Ending For Mrs. Sorken

If you should wish to do MRS. SORKEN separate from DURANG/DURANG, may I suggest another ending? Keep it the same up until the phrase "Now, to wrap up." Then we would just drop all the lines about what plays are to follow, but keep these other ones:

MRS. SORKEN.   Now to wrap up.

Dear theatergoers. I hope you enjoy your evening this evening. I'm not quite sure what you're seeing, but whatever it is, I'm sure it will be splendid.

And, by the way, if you are ever in Connecticut, I hope you will drop in and say hello to me and Mr. Sorken. He prefers that you call first, but I love to be surprised. So just ring the bell, and we'll have cocktails.

And I hope you have enjoyed my humbly offered comments on the drama. I have definitely enjoyed speaking with you, and have a sneaking suspicion that in the future, it is going to be harder and harder to shut me up.

(Either end with that, or possibly add and end with: "And so, the high point of my life to date being over, I leave you with the play.")

FOR WHOM THE
SOUTHERN BELLE TOLLS

About The Play

This play is a parody spin-off of Tennessee Williams' THE GLASS MENAGERIE. Audiences unfamiliar with the play seem able to enjoy it anyway — because parent-child tensions are the core theme of it — but the play is definitely geared to people who know the Williams play.

I've always had a strong reaction to THE GLASS MENAGERIE. I think it's quite a wonderful play. I first was captivated by the play in high school when I took home a recording of it from the library, which featured the stellar cast of Jessica Tandy as Amanda, Montgomery Clift as Tom, Julie Harris as Laura, and David Wayne as the Gentleman Caller. Tom's feeling trapped, Laura's feeling overwhelmed by the world (and typing class), and Amanda's trying to force them both to be other than who they were — these themes reverberated with me.

In graduate school at Yale School of Drama, however, I discovered that as I got older there was something in me that was starting to find the Amanda-Laura relationship funny — these two souls stuck together, one hopelessly trying to change the other one, who couldn't and wouldn't budge.

I befriended fellow playwright Albert Innaurato and we ended up writing a strange sketch based on MENAGERIE in which he played an over-bearing Amanda and I played a shy, withering Laura, but we didn't dress as women, we dressed as priests. Well, it made sense to us at the time.

Our take on MENAGERIE was about 7 minutes, and was exceptionally lunatic. (It became part of a cabaret act Albert and I did together called I DON'T GENERALLY LIKE POETRY BUT HAVE YOU READ "TREES"?)

I didn't think about MENAGERIE again until I saw yet another production in the mid-80s. I actually quite liked the production, but found that between the various movie and TV versions, a couple of high school productions, and some other stage ones, I felt over-exposed to the play. And though I still admired the play quite genuinely, I seemed to have reached that place where I found it hard to respond normally because I knew it too well.

And though I as a child always felt sympathy for Laura, as an adult I started to find Laura's sensitivity frustrating. I mean, how hard was typing class really?

And though in my youth I found Laura's interest in her glass animals to be sweet and other-worldly (with the appropriately perfect symbolism of her loving her glass unicorn best because it was different), now as an adult, I felt restless with her little hobby. Did she actually spend hours and hours staring at them? Couldn't she try to function in the world just a little bit? Why didn't she go out bowling, or make prank phone calls, or get drunk on a good bottle of bourbon?

Anyway, I started to find Laura annoying and frustrating.

It's out of this irritation with Laura's sensitivity — a feeling greatly at odds with the Williams original — that I seem to have written this parody, FOR WHOM THE SOUTHERN

BELLE TOLLS. (I say "seem" because I often say "seem"; and because I approached writing this parody on impulse, unaware consciously of how my feelings toward the play had changed. Writing the parody was a way of playing with, and releasing, some of what I felt after seeing the play for what seemed the 100th time.)

I've been happy that some of the critics have described this parody as "affectionate." I do feel affectionate toward the original play. But there is something about sweet, sensitive Laura that seems to have gotten on my nerves.

About Acting The Play

I've seen Amanda played a number of ways, all of which seemed to work.

It was a pleasure to watch Lizbeth Mackay's work on the role at Manhattan Theatre Club. Lizbeth was a fellow student at Yale School of Drama. As a dramatic actress, she's fluid and effortless and very moving. She brought all this same commitment to the comic exaggeration of my Amanda, and it deepened the play. Although the play remained very much a comedy, with Lizbeth doing the part we actually felt for this woman whose life seemed to be over. And because Lizbeth is still young and attractive, she was very believable as someone who would have other possibilities available if only she could unload her impossible son Lawrence.

Lizbeth was wonderfully convincing on the Southern charm; when she'd lecture Lawrence on it, she seemed to have real knowledge to impart.

And when the "feminine caller" arrived, her graciousness was an extremely funny starting place for her on-going realizations of how limited and odd Ginny turned out to be.

102

The director, Walter Bobbie, felt that playing the negative was a danger — if Amanda believed that there was *no* chance that this evening would work out for Lawrence, then the actress had nowhere to go and nothing to play. So, in a way, Walter's Amanda sort of played the same intention as the Amanda in the Williams' play: she's hoping that the "feminine caller" will work out and be a match for Lawrence, and will solve her "problem" for her.

I agree with Walter that playing the negative is dangerous; yet because the play is short (30 minutes about), if the actress has the right comic spin, I think a more despairing attitude can also work.

At the Tennessee Williams Literary Festival in New Orleans, I saw an actress named Ann Meric play Amanda in BELLE in a very different way that was still very funny. Older than Lizbeth, Ann played Amanda as clearly spent, fed-up, barely able to put up with either son for a moment longer. Because she has a low voice and comic timing, and because she said everything with real psychological truth, Ms. Meric made the story a darker one, but still very funny.

But whatever the choices are, the stakes must be high for Amanda. And when she and Tom fight at the end, it must be a full-out, emotional fight, much like the one in the Williams play.

About Lawrence

To casting directors, I ended up saying things like "we need a male Laura." Just as you would cast Laura in MENAGERIE as sweet and sensitive and appealing but a little odd, so I'd like to see those qualities in an actor playing Lawrence. Thus boyish and slight; preferably not effeminate, just "soft" in soul and aura. And with comic abilities. (Ah, the hard part.)

Lawrence is a hypochondriac, and he does believe in his ailments. He treasures his ailments.

Keith Reddin, who played Daisy for me in my BABY WITH THE BATHWATER in 1983, played Lawrence at MTC. He has the sweetness to be Lawrence, but he's also a little innately strange and off-beat. And he's boyish still. And he knows how to say odd things in a normal tone of voice, as if there's nothing remarkable about what he's saying. So it was a pleasure hooking up with him again.

About Tom

Tom is, frankly, a bit under-written and thus a little hard to play.

What we looked for in casting him was a "regular guy" who had a sexuality to him; we wanted to believe that he was out having a good time with sailors. And we also wanted someone who had the anger to play the "I'm going to the movies" argument with Amanda full out; and yet also would be believable in hitting the same sensitive sound in his "I didn't go to the moon" speech that an actor would need to play Tom in the Williams play. And who had the skill to fill in the less written parts — such as his kind of restlessness at home, mostly paying attention to what's going on, but wanting the dinner to be over so he can get to his adventure at the movies.

David Aaron Baker hit all these notes, and made an excellent Tom.

Tom's "other life" as a gay man is a minor note in this play, and obviously plays off of what we came to know about Tennessee Williams' own active sex life and the fact that Tom in MENAGERIE is acknowledged to be Williams' stand-in. So I just added our knowledge of that sex life to the MENAGERIE story. It's a joke, of course; but that's the basis of the joke.

And *Humpy Bus Boys* is one of my favorite movies.

About Ginny

Judging from auditions, Ginny appears to be a hard part sometimes for actors to figure out.

Ginny is a "regular guy" kind of girl and works at the factory with Lawrence's brother. She is hale and hearty, and also hard of hearing. She doesn't think she's hard of hearing, however. She thinks she hears fine. Also, she talks rather loudly — both out of enthusiasm and out of her hearing problem.

So for starters, the actress must speak loudly. You can't talk in a normal voice and then leave the actress playing Amanda stuck with the line "Why is she shouting? Is she deaf?" which then makes no sense.

On the other hand, if she speaks so loudly it hurts our ears, then we're in trouble. Likewise she shouldn't just shout but then forget to act the content and intention of her lines.

Walter worked with Patricia Randell on choosing when Ginny's speaking would be at its loudest (especially during her opening scene meeting everyone), and when it would be appropriate to have her talk in a more normal tone of voice (especially during her solo scene with Lawrence).

When she's talking in a normal level of loudness, it's not that she suddenly isn't hard of hearing. It's two things: it's a theatrical convention, where we're giving the audience a bit of a break; and it's identifying places in the text where it makes sense psychologically that Ginny is less emphatic, less excited.

Ginny is hard of hearing, but this is *not* a fact she acknowledges. So when she says "What?" to something someone's said, she doesn't in any way play that she thinks it's odd she didn't hear. It's just a fact, the person must have spoken too softly; she's enjoying the conversation immensely, so please tell her again what it is you said so she can keep enjoying the conversation.

Patricia Randell was especially good on her cheerful enjoyment of everything; her Ginny was a very happy person who tended to think wherever she was, people would like her and she would have fun. When she said "What?" loudly in her opening scene, she always had a happy excited smile on her face. And when people reacted in confusion to the things she said, she never, of course, noticed that. Ginny is in her own world; and she thinks she's just fine. She has no judgment of herself; and no knowledge that she mishears things.

(By the way, when she says "What?", keep the "Whats" as loud as the rest of what she says. In auditions, actresses sometimes would talk loudly, but then talk softly on the word "what?" It was a choice I didn't understand. If Ginny talks loudly unconsciously, as she does, then she would also be loud on her "What?")

One can choose to cast or play Ginny as fairly "butch," and costume her accordingly in, say, her factory clothes (like a garage mechanic's uniform or something).

Or you can go a less dead-on way, as we did with Patricia Randell. Patricia's Ginny was overly friendly and boisterous but not initially "butch." She was also dressed in a nice pants suit that one might wear to go to a stranger's house for dinner; a dress would be too feminine for Ginny to wear, but a pants suit seemed fine. And she wore a colored netting on the back of her hair, kind of 1940s ROSIE THE RIVETER style. (The costumes all gently pushed the time back to the time of the Williams play.)

When Ginny gets to showing Lawrence how to act "normal" ("The Braves played a helluva game, don'tcha think?"), at that point, though, she should be as butch as the actress can be.

And that's almost the limit of what there is for Ginny to play. When the evening's fallen to pieces, she can get quite angry at Lawrence and Amanda, but, strangely, her personality is so sunny that she gets over it fast. And on her exit she actually does mean that she had a really good time. She's a happy soul, she fits into the world comfortably — something she shares, in her exaggerated way, with the Gentleman Caller of the Williams play.

Miscellaneous Thought On The Swizzle Sticks

It's fun to choose these for Lawrence. And there turn out to be many more swizzle stick possibilities out in the world than one would think.

I prefer that only clear ones be used — either glass or plastic that looks like glass, to echo the glass menagerie comparison. If you choose any that are solid plastic, it looks wrong to me; or if you choose too many that have "hats" on them or too many little figurines. (A few figurines, if they're clear, are okay.)

Obviously when Lawrence comments on the colors of the swizzle sticks ("I call this one blue because it's blue"), they should be the colored glass he says they are.

But when he chooses, say, a swizzle stick and says he calls it "Q-tip" or "thermometer" because it looks like those objects, the joke ends up being funnier if the swizzle sticks look quite ordinary, so that it's his demented imagination that makes naming them "Q-tip" what's funny.

In one production, the prop person found a swizzle stick with large clear round "balls" on either end, and it *did* look like a Q-tip. The line then wasn't that funny because Lawrence's name for the stick seemed logical. When we then changed the prop to a normal size, conventional swizzle stick without the bulbous ends, then the line went back to getting a big laugh again.

Isn't comedy fascinating? It's both frustrating and intriguing how tiny things and gestures and intonations can change a line from getting a laugh to not getting a laugh.

Some Cuts For Belle

At MTC we wanted both acts to play at an hour, or a little under. So in previews we made a series of cuts in the texts. The initial cuts I was in total agreement with, and I've incorporated those cuts into these scripts. There was a final bunch of cuts we took in BELLE, however, that I didn't really like or feel comfortable with. But I include most of them here in case you find your Act One running too long.

1. Cut Amanda's "honey, that's part of your charm. Some days."

What remains would be:

LAWRENCE: I don't like the world, mama. I like it here in this room.

AMANDA: I know you do, Lawrence. But, honey, what about making a living?

2. Cut the following:

> AMANDA: That's lovely, Lawrence. You must tell us more over dinner.
> LAWRENCE: Alright.
> AMANDA: That was a *joke*, Lawrence.
> LAWRENCE: Don't try to make me laugh, mama. My asthma.

What remains would be:

> LAWRENCE: I have scabs from the itching, mama.
> AMANDA: Now, Lawrence, I don't want you talking about your ailments to the feminine caller ... (etc. as written.)

3. Cut Amanda's "honey, if you can't go out the door without getting an upset stomach or an attack of vertigo, then we got ..."

What remains, slightly re-worded, would be:

> LAWRENCE: It's unfeminine for a girl to work at a warehouse.
> AMANDA: Now, Lawrence, if we don't find some nice girl who's willing to support you, how am I ever going to get you out of this house and off my hands?

4. When Tom is banging on the door to get in, cut this brief exchange:

> AMANDA: Now you answer that door like any normal person.
> LAWRENCE: I can't.

A small change, but keeps it moving. This changes a cue for Tom.

5. Cut Amanda's off-stage phrase "or I'm going to give that over-bearing girl your *entire* collection of glass gobbledy-gook."

What remains would be:

> AMANDA: Now you get out of that bed this minute, Lawrence Wingvalley — is that clear?

6. Cut Lawrence's phrase, in his scene with Ginny, "I was always so afraid people were looking at me, and pointing." Also cut the word "eventually" in the next sentence.

What remains would be:

> GINNY: ... clumping up the aisle with this great big noisy leg brace on your leg. God, you made a racket.
> LAWRENCE: But then mama wouldn't let me wear the leg brace anymore. She gave it to the salvation army.

7. Cut Ginny's "I hope your rash gets better."

What remains would be:

GINNY: So long, Shakespeare. See you at the warehouse. So long, Lawrence.
LAWRENCE: You broke thermometer.

8. In Tom's "I didn't go to the moon" speech, one can cut the following phrases:

> Tom: "... it always caught me by surprise. Sometimes it would be a swizzle stick in someone's vodka glass, or sometimes it would just be a jar of pigs feet."

> ... "And of his collection of glass."

> ... "Or some other drug."

9. After Tom's exit, one can cut the following lines between Amanda and Lawrence (though this is the cut I like least):

Possible cut:

> LAWRENCE: Just lucky, mama.
> AMANDA: Don't make jokes, Lawrence. Your asthma. Your eczema. My life.
> LAWRENCE: Don't be sad, mama. We have each other for company and amusement.
> AMANDA: That's right. It's always darkest before the dawn. Or right before a typhoon sweeps up and kills everybody.

What remains would be:

> LAWRENCE: Look at the light through the glass, Mama. Isn't it amazin'?
> AMANDA: Yes, I guess it is, Lawrence. Oh, but both my children are weird. What have I done, O Lord, to deserve them?

LAWRENCE: Oh poor mama, let me try to cheer you up with my collection. Is that a good idea?

A STYE OF THE EYE

About The Play

This is a parody of Sam Shepard's play LIE OF THE MIND, with bits of some of his other plays thrown in for good measure. (And also with bits of David Mamet and John Pielmeier's AGNES OF GOD.)

Though critically acclaimed in 1985, LIE OF THE MIND turns out not to be that well known by audiences. So I feared that their not knowing the play would keep my parody from working.

However, the audience at Manhattan Theatre Club seemed happy to accept A STYE OF THE EYE as a parody of a certain kind of macho-poetic symbolic drama; and they seemed quite consistently willing to go with it and have a good time.

Though the parody is not as affectionate as the Williams one, still the point of doing the parody is to have the audience enjoy themselves, and to kind of jointly shake off some irritation from many an evening of pretentious, symbolic drama. (And not just Shepard.)

I wrote STYE a while ago, but added the character of Wesley (who's featured in CURSE OF THE STARVING CLASS) specifically for the Manhattan Theatre Club production because I knew that David Aaron Baker was going to be part of the acting company, and Walter Bobbie and I wanted STYE to feature all seven actors. So I chose a Shepard character to parody that would suit David's look and abilities. (David is late twenties, handsome, and a most versatile actor. I thought he would play well and comically the spacey, mind-elsewhere mysteriousness of Wesley. And he did.)

Writing the play, I enjoyed myself. Discussing it now, I feel somewhat guilty, in that I don't like putting myself in print in a critical role about a fellow dramatist. And I know how painful it is to receive criticism in the newspaper; and here I am offering it in print of another author. And I do admire several of Shepard's plays, especially CURSE OF THE STARVING CLASS, BURIED CHILD and FOOL FOR LOVE (play, not movie).

But LIE OF THE MIND really irritated me; and the critical kudos it received at the time baffled me, and discouraged me. (If this was acclaimed, how was I to fit into the New York theatre? was the thought that stopped me.)

So, blah blah blah. There you have it. But I hope the parody made you laugh.

About Acting The Play

About Ma:

The first few actresses (E. Katherine Kerr, Harriet Harris, Debra Monk) who read "Ma" in the life of this play seemed to get it dead-on perfect immediately, and they all also made approximately the same choices.

And at MTC Becky Ann Baker was outstanding as Ma, often getting applause at the end of her scene.

However, in auditions for MTC, about 75% of the good actresses who auditioned seemed to have trouble finding the part. So for that reason, I offer some clarifications.

Ma is feisty, straight-talkin', a no-nonsense lady who lives some-where out west. She don't fuss much, she says what's on her mind. She talks loud and bold. She swats mosquitoes on her forehead with the back of her hand, she sits unladylike but comfortable with her legs spread wide. She wears messy, loose print house dresses, with sneakers or boots or something that's comfortable to walk around the farm in.

I've also written, especially in the first scene, that she can't seem to remember anything.

I've already written this into a note in the text itself, but I'll repeat it: the comedy about her not remembering only works if you play Ma as totally forgetting from line to line. The first time her son Jake mentions his wife Beth, Ma asks: "Who's Beth?" Then a moment later Jake mentions Beth again, and Ma says: "Who's Beth?"

If you play it as if she half-remembers, and says the second "Who's Beth" with a twinge of "That name sound familiar, who is it again?", it just isn't funny. While if with feisty authority she keeps asking the same question over and over, with no self-knowledge and no uncertainty — then it is funny. (And it's also much more frustrating for Jake.)

In case it's helpful, the character of Ma reminds me of all the feisty Crackers that Marjorie Main played in the movies of the 1930s and 40s.

Probably only film buffs know Marjorie Main now, but in case you would find it helpful to look up her work on video, she played Ma Kettle in a series of films (starting with THE EGG AND I). Ma Kettle was kind of a hillbilly woman who was blunt with a twang and was a no-nonsense kind of gal; she and Pa had eleven to fifteen children, and she'd sort of cook in the kitchen with live chickens wandering about under foot. She spoke her mind, and wasn't afraid of anybody.

And she played similar characters in a number of other films, notably in the wonderful 1939 classic THE WOMEN, where she played unflappable Lucy, the woman who runs the Reno, Nevado ranch for divorced women (and where she doesn't blink an eye when Paulette Goddard and Rosalind Russell scratch and bite and tear one another's hair out; she calmly throws water on them, like they were a pair of dogs); and in a film I don't know called MURDER, HE SAYS, which Pauline Kael mentions favorably as a loony comedy about "homicidal hillbillies." Cracker, hillbilly — these words conjure up Marjorie Main, and what I have in mind for Ma.

So, if that's helpful, you might want to find an old movie on video or on TNT or AMC with Marjorie Main in it. (She also played "warmer" characters, like the loyal maid in MEET ME IN ST. LOUIS, but those parts don't help much with Ma.)

About Jake:

With Jake, it's good if you can find someone who's effortlessly masculine and has a good theatrical temper, the kind that's loud and angry and yet comes out funny.

In Shepard's LIE OF THE MIND there are two brothers: rabble-rouser problem kid Jake, and good, doe-eyed Frankie. I found the dichotomy between "bad" brother and "good" brother a little formulaic, and so in my parody I've put him into the same character.

However the actor chooses to switch between being Jake and being Frankie, the switch should be fast. Often just switching looks between the two characters can be enough: Jake talks to Frankie looking left, then switches to looking right as Frankie talks back to Jake. Or you can move your body a bit too, if that feels natural to you.

Frankie as the "good" brother does sound calmer than Jake and more reasoned, and yet in the first scene with Ma on the phone, good Frankie also has reason to get annoyed with Ma. So don't be afraid to let Frankie have an anger too; it doesn't rob them of difference ... they both have tempers, the whole family does; it's just Jake is a "rage-aholic" and Frankie only has a temper from time to time and is generally more reasonable.

Jake also has a crybaby side that I thought Marcus Giamatti brought out beautifully; one minute he'd be seething about why he had to beat Beth to death, the next minute he'd get all blubbery and weepy about feeling lonely that she was gone. (Just like a wife beater.)

The Mamet speech. Must be staccato and fast, the way Mamet dialogue usually is. Must be. Fast. Must be fast. You know what I mean? Fast? Quick? Are you stupid? Do you know? Am I right? Right! Fuckin' A.

A warning of something we found in rehearsal. Don't get stuck on how "Frankie" would sound doing the speech; just do it the way you would do the speech.

Marcus in rehearsal first did the speech great, then he seemed to get lost; and for a while we couldn't figure out what was wrong. Then finally it came out it had to do with trying to do the Mamet speech in "Frankie's" voice.

As Jake and Frankie, Marcus was using a bit of a western drawl, which sounded good. But this drawl elongated his vowel sounds a bit, and these longer vowels slowed the rhythm in the Mamet speech, and made the speech seem slow and un-Mametlike. So Walter and I gave him permission not to worry about sounding like Frankie during the speech; but just to do it in his own voice, in the quick rhythms he initially used instinctively.

It's not that I want the GLENGARRY GLEN ROSS parody to sound different from Frankie .... but if anything is stopping you from being staccato and fast on the Mamet speech, let go of it. (When Marcus changed his interpretation in preview to the faster rhythms, the audience laughter and recognition improved enormously.)

Beth's Language After Being Brain-Damaged:

I've written a lot of nonsense syllables for Beth to say when she comes out of the hospital.

Walter found it helpful to get Keith Reddin to work on making the nonsense syllables make inner sense to him, if not to the audience. So, for instance, with Beth's first long list of "Mummy. Mommy. Custom. Costume. Capsule. Cupcake" etc., Keith played it that he was telling his mother of all the things he saw at the hospital. Or he was free-associating from his days in the theatre to the hospital to now. The audience still heard nonsense, of course; but it was good to make it seem that Beth knew what she was talking about.

And Keith also would play and hold onto any specific acting intention he could find. So, for instance, once Beth says "I want Jake," upon meeting Frankie, it's quite possible to keep relating everything to wanting Jake, to checking Frankie out to make sure he isn't Jake, etc. etc.

Meg, Mae And Wesley:

Meg in LIE OF THE MIND was played by Ann Wedgeworth, and my version of Meg was very much based on her amusing, likable performance. Meg is kind of sexy, and very vague; life is in a haze to her. Her look is important: sexy tight jeans (or stretch pants), a kind of trashy, off-the-shoulder blouse or sweater. Sexy red hair if possible.

117

When Mae shows up seductively as Jake-Frankie's sister, she is a parody character from a different Shepard play, FOOL FOR LOVE. And in the Shepard-directed version of that play in New York, the brother-sister lovers were wildly and humorously intense. They would embrace passionately, then separate, and pretty much hurl themselves against opposite walls, stare at one another, panting and exhausted, then rush back at one another again. (This was quite funny actually, and effective in communicating their weird passion for one another. I liked FOOL FOR LOVE on stage.)

So, anyway, that's why my parody characters of Mae and Jake-Frankie throw themselves around that way.

And when Wesley comes in just wearing underpants, that's because in Shepard's CURSE OF THE STARVING CLASS a character named Wesley suddenly wanders about the house totally naked but somewhat inexplicably carrying an ailing sheep. Wesley marches to his own drummer, and has slow, deep thoughts that we can only imagine.

Many (most?) in the audience don't get these specific references; but as I said earlier, they seemed to enjoy going for the ride anyway. It's a Weird Poetic-Symbolism Play parody.

Finally, Wesley's last speech: "There are three different words in artichoke. There's 'art.' And there's 'choke.' And there's 'ih.'"

That speech should be done With Importance and Emphasis. But it seems to be important how you say "ih." When David Aaron Baker did it, it seemed to work best when he was his most emphatic and important on the word "ih"; and when "ih" had the feeling of the sound you make when you go "ugh" or "bleccch" to something you don't like.

Well, I think enough notes on STYE. I'm tiring myself out.

NINA IN THE MORNING

On The Play

This play began as a short story.

When Manhattan Theatre Club approached me and Walter Bobbie about doing an evening of one act plays of mine, I knew I had FOR WHOM THE SOUTHERN BELLE TOLLS and A STYE OF THE EYE available for such an evening. But both of those are theatre parodies, and I had worries about whether a whole evening of theatre parody would wear out its welcome. (A few years earlier, a friend, John Money, had wanted to produce an evening of theatre parody by me, and to call it DERANGED THEATRICS. I consented, but then got cold feet and withdrew. I became fearful of how the critics would treat such a "light" off-Broadway evening from me. And I didn't think I had a "full" evening of theatre parody in me. And I was starting to go through a "fear of the New York *Times* critic" phase.)

Well, so anyway, it was my belief that Act Two should not be theatre parody.

And so Walter and I looked at this short story of mine, and decided it could be easily adapted to stage.

The style of the story was part of its effect; and so I created a Narrator, so he could speak in the story's style.

I owe Walter Bobbie a debt of gratitude for his inventive staging of this piece. I had envisioned Nina being quite stationary for most of the piece, but Walter had her moving up and about, especially when she was in memory; and this staging helped enliven the piece, and let us go in and out of memory with Nina most vividly.

119

I wrote that Nina's children James and Robert would be played by the same actor. The Narrator also mentions Nina's daughter, and I intended to write something to allow for the same actor to play her as well. But before I got to do that, Walter devised a way for the daughter character to enter, using the existing narration. His idea enlivened what I'd already written, and took care of the need of my having to add something for the daughter.

Anyway, I thought his work was especially outstanding in this piece.

NINA is not a parody. It is meant to be its own thing. At MTC, because Act One consisted of a monologue about theatre and two theatre parodies, I was alarmed to learn that many people were racking their brains during NINA trying to figure out what it was a parody of. Was it Edward Albee? (The formality of the language and the wealth of the people suggested him a bit.) Was it Noel Coward? Was it the performance art of Robert Wilson? (Some of Walter's staging suggested Wilson a little bit.) What was it?

My mention in the program that Act One was Theatre, Act Two was Everything Else was clearly too subtle. Plus lots of people don't read the program.

So late in the run, one afternoon I talked with the actresses backstage about the problem, and said I had thought about giving Mrs. Sorken a line explaining to the audience that Act Two was not theatre parodies. Patricia Elliott (who played Nina as well as Mrs. Sorken) jumped at this and was extremely game — she was willing to try a new line in the middle of her speech that very afternoon in 10 minutes. So I gave her a couple of possibilities, all fine, but a little convoluted. But, strangely, when she tried to repeat them back, she came up with her own abridged version that went: "Act One is theatre parodies. Act Two ... is not."

Given her elaborate manner of speaking, the blunt inelegance of this phrasing seemed funny to us in the dressing room. And then to the audience a few moments later. So I've written it in. And it seemed to help. I wish I had thought to put it in earlier in the run.

(Yes, I know that the proper grammar would be "Act One is theatre parody." But I think the audience hears better "Act One is theatre parodies"; and so that's how I've left it.)

On Producing And Acting Nina In The Morning

The look of the play, Walter and I decided, should be like a Calvin Klein "Obsessions" ad. At first we thought that meant black and white. But the designer David Woolard put Nina in a stunning off-the-shoulder bright red evening gown, with a comically long train, and with her hair slicked fashionably back and off her face. She sort of looked like the Wicked Queen in SNOW WHITE meets Calvin Klein.

Walter added the presence of a maid, to add atmosphere and to help Foote move certain props.

If Calvin Klein's "Obsessions" is one way to think of the play, another one is to think of the drawings and stories of Edward Gorey — all those thin creatures with long dresses and capes, who stand around staring dispassionately, while awful tragedies occur one after another around them.

For music we wanted beautiful and mysterious, perhaps an opera aria. We ended up using a lovely aria for two sopranos from the opera LAKME* by Delibes. This aria has gotten a bit popular because it's used in an ad for British Airlines; and it was used in the vampire movie THE HUNGER (and is on

---

* See Special Note on Songs and Recordings on copyright page.

that movie's soundtrack recording). There are, I'm sure, other ones too. (Rachmanioff's "Vocalise"* for a soprano voice might be another.)

I think it's important to mime the facelift-pins-in-the-face stuff; I think miming it adds to the stylization and distancing that the piece needs.

When I wrote it, I envisioned Nina sitting still for the whole thing, with the Narrator's lines telling us what she thinking. I think that would still work. Though I really enjoyed what Walter Bobbie brought to the staging, with Nina walking to different parts of the stage with different memories.

There was an early part in rehearsal where it was all movement and flow, and it was hard to follow and enjoy. (Luckily, this was an early rehearsal, not a preview.) And one of the things that had gotten lost in this rehearsal was the clarity of events in Nina's mind.

Much of the play takes place on a *particular day*: on that particular day, Nina's facelift has fallen; her son James has said he hates her and tried to take pins out of her face; her son Robert has shot her in the shoulder; and she has asked for a cruller which she has not received. It is those events which are current and happening now which bring her to the point at the end of the play where she is legitimately considering whether she wants to continue living or not, whether to have "lunch or death."

All the other things that happen are memories from the past; Nina can and should lose herself in them, but whenever she comes back to a moment in the present day, it's important for the actress to keep in mind that these present-day events

---

* See Special Note on Songs and Recordings on copyright page.

are what her major journey is in the play, short though it is. The other things are flashbacks, meant to inform the audience and to comfort and distract Nina. But the present-day events must not be forgotten; they add up for Nina.

Sorry about line readings, but the last line "death or lunch" is important to me. Please don't go for any easy humor of saying "death" portentously and then "lunch" lightly or cutely.

Nina takes herself so seriously that, I think, she would intone both options with equal seriousness, giving both equal weight. It's the giving of equal weight to these ludicrously unequal things that makes the line funny and strange.

Patricia Elliott was very special, funny and scary as Nina. Like me, she hadn't done theatre for a few years; so it was a real pleasure for me to have her come back in this role and the other ones she played in this evening.

Oh, a minor note, about the monk. Walter had Keith, who played all three children, play the monk. But the monk wore a large brown robe with an over-sized cowl that totally covered his head and face, so the audience never knew it was Keith. I liked not seeing the monk's face, and I offer that as a possible way of handling it. (If you did let the monk's face be seen, then choose a different actor, not the actor playing Foote or playing the children.)

WANDA'S VISIT

About The Play

This play is based on a teleplay I wrote in 1986 for a PBS half-hour comedy series called *Trying Times,* created by Jon Denny. It was Denny's idea to ask various playwrights to write half-hour teleplays about "difficult times." Denny produced about 12 of them for WCET in Los Angeles. The first ones included Beth Henley on meeting the in-laws; Wendy Wasserstein on learning to drive; Bernard Slade on moving day; George C. Wolfe on having a black maid put a spell on your house; Albert Innaurato on dealing with a tax audit. (The *Trying Times,* programs show up from time to time on PBS stations, and make fun watching.)

My episode was number six, and my topic was dealing with a visit from someone from your high school days.

The character of Wanda — needy, manipulative, impossible to be rid of — came charging out of my brain, and was great fun to write.

The teleplay was filmed in a week, directed by Alan Arkin, and starring Jeff Daniels, Julie Hagerty and Swoosie Kurtz as Wanda.

My professional path had crossed Swoosie's when she played Bette in my play A HISTORY OF THE AMERICAN FILM at Arena Stage in 1977, and then repeated her role in 1978 on Broadway, winning a Drama Desk award for her portrayal. And in 1977 she also played the pivotal, comic role of Rita in my friend Wendy Wasserstein's play UNCOMMON WOMEN AND OTHERS, both on-stage and on camera for PBS's *Great Performances.*

Swoosie is a very special comic talent, and it was a thrill to have her play Wanda. Indeed this whole experience of working with Jeff, Julie, Swoosie and Alan was one of the nicest, and most artistically successful, professional experiences I've had. (And for added fun, I played the role of the Waiter. Nepotism. Authorism?)

I was sorry that more people didn't see it (and there's occasionally talk about putting some of the *Trying Times* out on video; I wish they would). So I decided to re-present it onstage as part of DURANG/DURANG.

The script is mostly the dialogue from the teleplay. I have made some changes for transition purposes. For instance, on film we could simply fade to later in the evening, with Wanda wrapped in a blanket, talking, talking. On stage, I had to find other ways to make time pass.

And as I was adapting it, some new lines also came to me; and often I included those as well. (Marsha got some new quirks in the restaurant scene.)

About Producing And Acting The Play

This play is a real relationship piece. Sometimes it was a little hard for the audience to shift gears to get into it because it's in a very different style than the first four plays in DURANG/DURANG; but once they did shift I felt they all identified with the familiar feelings about marriage and about long-term relationships. And on the best nights I felt they were highly amused, and alarmed, by Wanda; and very much rooted for Marsha, the realist, who wanted this nut out of there.

"Nut" is a dangerous word, though. I think Wanda should be fun and have her charm; that's part of what Jim responds to (though primarily he's responding to her flirting with him;

he's hungry for someone to think he's special at this point in his life).

But Wanda's very selfish, and has literally no ability to wonder how anyone else is feeling. And she finds her own story fascinating, and assumes everyone else will too.

Wanda mentions her weight early on; and then there are references to food as well. In the TV version, Swoosie Kurtz, who is very thin, did all the same lines about feeling she looked heavy; and they worked in that version as the diet-obsessed chatter of a thin woman. We all know some of those thin women who think they have a weight problem, when they don't.

When we auditioned for stage, however, Walter and I decided that as long as we were doing a new version, we wanted to see what it was like with heavier actresses in the role. And we ended up liking what happened when a somewhat overweight actress read for the part ... somehow Wanda is so needy, that it sort of fit that she "feed" her anxiety with food.

In terms of casting, it's important though that it be believable that Wanda likes sex, and has had a lot of it. Sometimes being overweight is a way of keeping oneself protected from sex (sorry to be an amateur psychologist) and sometimes it isn't; so it's important in terms of casting that Wanda be convincing in her flirtations and in her desires.

Because of the three-quarter thrust stage, it was kind of impossible to lug furniture on to change from scene to scene; so Walter and the designer Derek McLane chose to be really simple — three somewhat fancy dining room chairs and one round table — and they arranged the chairs to stand in for everything: chairs in the living room, and, most stylized, the bed in the bedroom (by bringing two chairs together, having the actors sit down and then throw a comforter over themselves).

I thought this was a good solution; and the few set pieces also made for a "light" feeling, where the setting was secondary to the characters and their interactions.

If you had a wider stage, and could have different playing areas with furniture already set up; or if you had ways of getting furniture on and off quickly — I think other solutions would be fine too. But the one we had worked for MTC.

We ended up miming all the food; and using glasses that were dark colored glass (or plastic) so you wouldn't be aware if there was liquid in them or not.

We did, though, use real crackers for Wanda to munch on; and that meant having a prop pate as well.

So our choice ended up being inconsistent (though I don't think the audience cared one way or another).

If you feel you want to deal with real food in the restaurant and at their dinner, I don't object. But we thought it was too difficult to do; and I hate making actors eat night after night onstage; and I also like things to happen quickly. So miming the food may be best.

For the two henchmen at the end (who work for the "kingpin"): we ended up using Keith and Patricia, but with both playing men. And with pants, raincoats, fedoras and large machine guns, you never had a sense that it wasn't two men.

The henchman should happen fast.

I think it's obvious from the script, but Jim and Marsha are both nice, intelligent people. Jim is feeling bored and restless, Marsha's feeling sort of ignored and left out. During their speeches at the beginning and the end, I think we should want things to work out for the two of them; they seem well suited, actually, and to care for one another. But I was pleased, in both the TV version and the stage version, that Marsha's and Jim's last two lines seemed very right and a little sad.

The play is a fun challenge for actors, I think; and Lizbeth Mackay, Marcus Giamatti and Becky Ann Baker as Wanda all did splendid jobs. Wanda, of course, is the showiest part, and we were lucky to have found Becky, who was charming and scary and very very funny.

BUSINESS LUNCH AT
THE RUSSIAN TEA ROOM

About The Play

I wrote this playlet directly for DURANG/DURANG.

It's about a playwright, named Chris, having a meeting with a film development person for a possible screenwriting job.

It's not a deep piece, and many writers have had their go at how Hollywood treats writers and thoughts and ideas — for instance, David Mamet's SPEED-THE-PLOW, John Patrick Shanley's FOUR DOGS AND A BONE, Arthur Kopit's ROAD TO NIRVANA (which started as a parody of the Mamet play and once had the loonier title of BONE-THE-FISH). And Christopher Guest's movie THE BIG PICTURE with Kevin Bacon as a young filmmaker getting jerked around on his first film was quite funny.

Writers have a history of hating working with Hollywood. My favorite example is J.D. Salinger. He sold his short story "Uncle Wiggily in Connecticut" to the movies, and they turned it into a soggy love story called *My Foolish Heart* (1949). He was so horrified that he vowed never to sell another thing to Hollywood, ever. And he never has. (And he lives in seclusion in Vermont. And he only speaks three sentences a day, two of them to his dog. No, I made up that last sentence.)

I'm more willing for things to work out with Hollywood and me, but so far, it's been disappointing. I wrote a screenplay with Wendy Wasserstein that wasn't made. I wrote many versions of SISTER MARY IGNATIUS EXPLAINS IT ALL FOR YOU for an independent producer, but funding could never be completed. I wrote a screenplay for Warner Bros. I'm very proud of, a Monty Python-esque comedy called THE NUN WHO SHOT LIBERTY VALANCE, which I keep wishing someone would make into a film. And the only script of mine that was filmed was a disaster: an unfunny, forced version of my play BEYOND THERAPY, which the director Robert Altman radically rewrote; I wish I had taken my name off of it, but I didn't. If ever you see it, I apologize.

My only happy writing experience, so far, in films was being hired to rewrite some of the scenes in the Michael J. Fox movie SECRET OF MY SUCCESS. I had a supporting role in that film, and I was asked to rewrite certain scenes a day or so before they were scheduled to shoot. It sounded intimidating, but it ended up being fun, and I like the scenes I wrote, and think it's a good commercial movie, directed by Herbert Ross, whom I enjoyed working with.

So I keep hoping I'll hook up with the right director, and the right project, and so on.

But many of my experiences (and those of my writer friends) have been writing for "development" people.

In this play, the character of Melissa Stearn is a "development person" — that is, her job is to "develop" projects and ideas into movies or TV movies or TV series.

I hope to work in movies and TV again (especially in New York, the non-earthquake capital of the world), so I want to admit and stress that I do not regard all development people with disdain.

But there have been some. "Ideas" for movies are so debatable. And many development people seem to have no background in writing, directing or acting ... they seem to have studied Opinion in college, and then they proclaim their opinions about "what works" and "what can't work" in a screenplay with total self-confidence.

And they want everything in outline form. I'm afraid I don't think (or create) in outline form. Do you?

But I see many a movie where I can recognize the outline, but it's not abetted by any good dialogue, any interesting character development, indeed any actual writing talent anywhere, just this damn outline that sounded good at the meeting.

From so many of these "outline" movies something vital is missing: the actual human desire to communicate is not there. What's replaced it is the desire to make money, and then, rather pathetically, to judge success by how expensive your car is, or your watch, or what restaurant you eat in. The Catholic school boy in me (and the writer) disapproves of this materialism. I like to earn money, but it's pretty far from my *sole* interest in life.

So maybe I should move to Vermont and talk to a dog. Salinger, by the way, was right about MY FOOLISH HEART, it isn't very good. Most of it is a flashback to what might have happened *before* the short story begins. However, the first 10 minutes are rather close to the story, and Susan Hayward is quite good for that brief section in capturing the story's bitter, edgy take on an unhappy, alcoholic woman. And the theme song is quite pretty.

Maybe Melissa Stearn can convince Salinger to finally let CATCHER IN THE RYE become a movie. In a few years Macauley Culken will be old enough. And I'd like to play Madame Arcati.

About Producing And Acting Russian Tea Room

Chris should be polite, and also have trouble saying no. He finds it embarrassing to say something is a bad idea, so he says things like "ah" and "I can see why you want to do it."

Margaret's part is small, but she's crisp, lively, she knows her client well and cares about him; she's just a trifle scattered and gets names wrong.

Melissa is very sure of herself, she loves her job, she loves her opinions, she's very much "in the business" and loves throwing around the names of Meg Ryan and Nora Ephron.

When she has her long speeches, usually telling a movie idea, she is always energetic, she enjoys telling the idea, she thinks they're always great. On a line like "he disappeared just like Julia Roberts did in that movie watchamacallit," don't slow down and get lost in thought, trying to think what it was, or feeling momentarily uncertain. She's a happy, fast-talking executive, and she breezes by "watchmacallit," it doesn't stop her; she assumes you know the one she means, and titles are only details anyway, she doesn't get bogged down in mere details.

When Chris says to Melissa "Funny, but you don't sound like a real person," Walter Bobbie directed Patricia Randell to just accept the comment without taking any offense; somehow she is beyond being insulted. And I thought that was very right.

To side-track with praise for a moment: Patricia Randell was an actress new to me whom Walter and I auditioned for Ginny for FOR WHOM THE SOUTHERN BELLE TOLLS at Ensemble Studio Theatre. Then when we cast again in the six-play DURANG/DURANG, we were delighted by the range she showed. And she was really funny as Melissa, automatically knowing the rhythm within which to speak (a pretty fast one, but she could also go off on another tack, momentarily wallowing in hatred for her mother, for instance).

And it was a pleasure to have Keith Reddin, a fellow playwright, stand in for me. Chris was his "low key" role in the evening, having been hilarious as the hypochondriacal Lawrence, very peculiar and funny as Agnes-Beth, and quite inspired as poor retarded La-La.

The Priest And Rabbi; The Ending

In the earliest draft of this, there was no final scene with the Rabbi and the Priest showing up; Chris just folded socks on his own, and he didn't have a fantasy about what he'd write. We were going to originally end with WANDA'S VISIT, but that ending seemed too thoughtful a tone to send the audience home on. So then we decided that BUSINESS LUNCH in its lightness and punchiness seemed the proper way to conclude the evening. But I needed to end it more satisfactorily than I had. So then I came up with the rabbi-priest variation on the ending.

When the Priest and the Rabbi break into disco dancing, I was in seventh heaven; and most of the audience was too. It was truly loony.

A couple of things about this section. Please don't make the Priest talk in an Irish accent; that is a cliché that is way past being funny, at least to me. I know I have him talking to "Mrs. McGillicutty"; that's because most of the Catholics I grew up around in my youth in the late 50s were Irish; *none* of them, though, spoke in an Irish accent.

To me the real joke of the Priest is how "Hollywood" he is: he's handsome, he's well-spoken, he's charming, he's all a leading man character should be. Then when the Rabbi comes out, dressed so other-worldly and never ever presented in a sexual way, it's partially that juxtaposition that's funny; he's not in any way a Hollywood fantasy.

I initially planned to have the Rabbi be played by a man; it is, after all, a gay affair between the Priest and the Rabbi that Melissa wants written.

However, we only had three actors at our disposal, and all three had parts already. We could have brought Marcus back, who had played the Waiter, but somehow it seemed wrong in the world of this play to have any actors double in parts. You didn't want the audience to have a moment of looking at the Rabbi and going: oh, right, he was the Waiter a minute ago.

So we cast Lizbeth Mackay in the part, who was the Southern mother in BELLE, poor white trash Meg in STYE, and strait-laced Marsha in WANDA'S VISIT. And now the Rabbi. Talk about stretching yourself in an evening!

There was something fun about including the role of the Rabbi in the trans-gender casting that had happened throughout the evening, especially in STYE where Beth is meant to be played by a young man. So if you want to also cast a woman as a rabbi, that's fine. Just be sure to give her a beard and a big black hat.

Casting a woman, though, did lower the emotional "shock" about the gay romance. So if you do the evening with more than 3 men, and want to consider a man as the rabbi, that's how I originally envisioned it.

Folding The Laundry

The ending, about folding the laundry. I don't want it to be a "down" ending. It's a strangely happy ending. In Chris' world he may have lost a good-paying job — that he felt mixed about anyway — but now he doesn't have to listen to Melissa's opinions anymore; and he's going to do, as he says, "what's simple and true. I'm going to fold my laundry."

At this moment in time folding the laundry represents something good, valuable and worth doing in his universe.

When the two characters break the convention of being in his head and offer to help, he's pleased to get their help.

I thought the ending was going to just be the somewhat sweet image of the three of them matching the socks together. But in tech rehearsal it became clear that for whatever reason actually making a match with a sock was hard. And so the ending shifted to the rather funny sight of these three people — Chris, Priest, and Rabbi — dutifully going through socks, holding them up together, not finding a match, and then going on to look for the next pair.

So I recommend playing that they're having trouble making a match (and thus there have to be lots of socks, to make this believable). Don't then "color" this difficulty matching with too much upset or frustration, just a little … they continue on with their resolve to do this "simple and true" thing; it's just that we see that their task is a little harder than we at first thought.

And, finally, I think the music you choose to fade out on at the end is important.

Walter came up with Irving Berlin's "It's a Lovely Day Today,"* which was perfect. It was upbeat but not frenetic, the lyric was quickly and easily understood; it also left the audience in a good mood (as did the last few beats of the play itself). (Reminder: you have get permission to use copyrighted music.)

Other choices are possible. But whatever you choose, the ending should be pleasantly upbeat, contented.

* See Special Note on Songs and Recordings on copyright page.

SCENE CHANGES

There are six plays, three per act. It's very important that any scene changes *within* a play be very quick and simple.

But there are also setting changes between the plays themselves, and these changes must be well rehearsed and as simple as possible. Strangely, we found that it was fine that the changes between plays not be instantaneous; the audience seemed to need a breath or two to change gears for the next play.

At MTC the music and sound during the changes between the plays seemed really important. The music chosen helped get the audience in the right mood for what they were about to see.

I'll give a couple of examples.

Mrs. Sorken's speech ended with a triumphant orchestral flourish that led into a blackout. She exited in dark, and as the scene change into FOR WHOM THE SOUTHERN BELLE started, a honky-tonk-ish Southern jazz music sneaked in at a low level, then upped to normal level. This effectively set the mood for the next play — it was upbeat, but not frenetic; the Dixieland jazz suggested the dance hall across the way in THE GLASS MENAGERIE, or at least something faintly Southern. And it gave the audience something to listen to while the few furniture pieces were brought on.

(MTC's Stage II is a thrust, three-quarters stage. Thus all furniture pieces had to be carried out by stage-hands or actors, in partial light. Rehearsing the changes until they were smooth, ordered, and brief was important.)

Once the BELLE set was in place, the jazz music and the lights faded out together.

Then in the dark we heard the delicate sound of tinkling glass — helping to set the "delicate" mood of the play (and of the original MENAGERIE); then a special light came up on Lawrence's special collection of glass cocktail stirrers, atop a special table. (This light cue often got a laugh.)

And then the rest of the stage lights came up, the tinkling glass sound cue faded down and out, the special on the "cocktail stirrers" faded down to normal stage light; and the play proper began, with Amanda's entrance.

I give that somewhat exhaustive description to indicate how important music and lights are to the scene changes; and how carefully they must be timed.

I'll describe one more set change between plays, and then let you figure out your own for the plays after that.

At the end of BELLE, as Amanda and Lawrence sit on the sofa together, Walter Bobbie brought in sad music underneath, and then the lights faded to black. (And the actors exited in dark.)

In early preview, we left the sad music on for much of the following scene change, but it was too much of a downer and an energy-robber.

So Walter changed it ... we kept the sad music for the fade out only, but during the applause we changed to the upbeat jazz music from earlier again. We couldn't risk the sad music enervating the audience.

Then once the BELLE furniture was cleared, the jazz (Dixieland) music faded out. (It felt as if when the BELLE furniture was on, one had to play music that related to the world of that play still.)

With the jazz music gone, we had momentary silence; then we heard the sound of desolate, whistling wind; then the sound of coyotes howling in the distance was added. Then the first prop was brought in: a large truck tire, placed on the floor.

Sometimes the audience giggled at how large the change in tone was — which was a good reaction.

The six plays all have very distinct tones and styles, and it's good to let the music help you switch from tone to tone.

THE ACTORS

I very much like working with actors. It's one of the pleasures for me in writing for theatre (and when I end up having some acting jobs of my own).

Working with the excellent actors I've been lucky enough to hook up with, I find that they either do the roles exactly as I had them in my head, or they sometimes do them even better. And when a "moment" gets lost — because repeating things is a difficult thing to do; or sometimes you change something subtle and you don't even know it — I even enjoy talking through and working through what went wrong and how to get it back.

Anyway, I'd like to thank the seven actors in DURANG/ DURANG again: Becky Ann Baker, David Aaron Baker (no relation, by the way), Patricia Elliott, Marcus Giamatti, Lizbeth Mackay, Patricia Randell, Keith Reddin.

Christopher Durang
August 1995
New York City

NEW PLAYS

★ **THE CREDEAUX CANVAS by Keith Bunin.** A forged painting leads to tragedy among friends. "There is that moment between adolescence and middle age when being disaffected looks attractive. Witness the enduring appeal of Prince Hamlet, Jake Barnes and James Dean, on the stage, page and screen. Or, more immediately, take a look at the lithe young things in THE CREDEAUX CANVAS..." *—NY Times.* "THE CREDEAUX CANVAS is the third recent play about painters...it turned out to be the best of the lot, better even than most plays about non-painters." *—NY Magazine.* [2M, 2W] ISBN: 0-8222-1838-0

★ **THE DIARY OF ANNE FRANK by Frances Goodrich and Albert Hackett, newly adapted by Wendy Kesselman.** A transcendently powerful new adaptation in which Anne Frank emerges from history a living, lyrical, intensely gifted young girl. "Undeniably moving. It shatters the heart. The evening never lets us forget the inhuman darkness waiting to claim its incandescently human heroine." *—NY Times.* "A sensitive, stirring and thoroughly engaging new adaptation." *—NY Newsday.* "A powerful new version that moves the audience to gasps, then tears." *—A.P.* "One of the year's ten best." *—Time Magazine.* [5M, 5W, 3 extras] ISBN: 0-8222-1718-X

★ **THE BOOK OF LIZ by David Sedaris and Amy Sedaris.** Sister Elizabeth Donderstock makes the cheese balls that support her religious community, but feeling unappreciated among the Squeamish, she decides to try her luck in the outside world. "...[a] delightfully off-key, off-color hymn to clichés we all live by, whether we know it or not." *—NY Times.* "Good-natured, goofy and frequently hilarious..." *—NY Newsday.* "...[THE BOOK OF LIZ] may well be the world's first Amish picaresque...hilarious..." *—Village Voice.* [2M, 2W (doubling, flexible casting to 8M, 7W)] ISBN: 0-8222-1827-5

★ **JAR THE FLOOR by Cheryl L. West.** A quartet of black women spanning four generations makes up this hilarious and heartwarming dramatic comedy. "...a moving and hilarious account of a black family sparring in a Chicago suburb..." *—NY Magazine.* "...heart-to-heart confrontations and surprising revelations...first-rate..." *—NY Daily News.* "...unpretentious good feelings...bubble through West's loving and humorous play..." *—Star-Ledger.* "...one of the wisest plays I've seen in ages...[from] a master playwright." *—USA Today.* [5W] ISBN: 0-8222-1809-7

★ **THIEF RIVER by Lee Blessing.** Love between two men over decades is explored in this incisive portrait of coming to terms with who you are. "Mr. Blessing unspools the plot ingeniously, skipping back and forth in time as the details require...an absorbing evening." *—NY Times.* "...wistful and sweet-spirited..." *—Variety.* [6M] ISBN: 0-8222-1839-9

★ **THE BEGINNING OF AUGUST by Tom Donaghy.** When Jackie's wife abruptly and mysteriously leaves him and their infant daughter, a pungently comic reevaluation of suburban life ensues. "Donaghy holds a cracked mirror up to the contemporary American family, anatomizing its frailties and miscommunications in fractured language that can be both funny and poignant." *—The Philadelphia Inquirer.* "...[A] sharp, eccentric new comedy. Pungently funny...fresh and precise..." *—LA Times.* [3M, 2W] ISBN: 0-8222-1786-4

★ **OUTSTANDING MEN'S MONOLOGUES 2001–2002 and OUTSTANDING WOMEN'S MONOLOGUES 2001–2002 edited by Craig Pospisil.** Drawn exclusively from Dramatists Play Service publications, these collections for actors feature over fifty monologues each and include an enormous range of voices, subject matter and characters. MEN'S ISBN: 0-8222-1821-6 WOMEN'S ISBN: 0-8222-1822-4

DRAMATISTS PLAY SERVICE, INC.
440 Park Avenue South, New York, NY 10016 212-683-8960 Fax 212-213-1539
postmaster@dramatists.com www.dramatists.com

NEW PLAYS

★ **A LESSON BEFORE DYING by Romulus Linney, based on the novel by Ernest J. Gaines.** An innocent young man is condemned to death in backwoods Louisiana and must learn to die with dignity. "The story's wrenching power lies not in its outrage but in the almost inexplicable grace the characters must muster as their only resistance to being treated like lesser beings." *—The New Yorker.* "Irresistable momentum and a cathartic explosion…a powerful inevitability." *—NY Times.* [5M, 2W] ISBN: 0-8222-1785-6

★ **BOOM TOWN by Jeff Daniels.** A searing drama mixing small-town love, politics and the consequences of betrayal. "…a brutally honest, contemporary foray into classic themes, exploring what moves people to lie, cheat, love and dream. By BOOM TOWN's climactic end there are no secrets, only bare truth." *—Oakland Press.* "…some of the most electrifying writing Daniels has ever done…" *—Ann Arbor News.* [2M, 1W] ISBN: 0-8222-1760-0

★ **INCORRUPTIBLE by Michael Hollinger.** When a motley order of medieval monks learns their patron saint no longer works miracles, a larcenous, one-eyed minstrel shows them an outrageous new way to pay old debts. "A lightning-fast farce, rich in both verbal and physical humor." *—American Theatre.* "Everything fits snugly in this funny, endearing black comedy…an artful blend of the mock-formal and the anachronistically breezy…A piece of remarkably dexterous craftsmanship." *—Philadelphia Inquirer.* "A farcical romp, scintillating and irreverent." *—Philadelphia Weekly.* [5M, 3W] ISBN: 0-8222-1787-2

★ **CELLINI by John Patrick Shanley.** Chronicles the life of the original "Renaissance Man," Benvenuto Cellini, the sixteenth-century Italian sculptor and man-about-town. Adapted from the autobiography of Benvenuto Cellini, translated by J. Addington Symonds. "[Shanley] has created a convincing Cellini, not neglecting his dark side, and a trim, vigorous, fast-moving show." *—BackStage.* "Very entertaining…With brave purpose, the narrative undermines chronology before untangling it…touching and funny…" *—NY Times.* [7M, 2W (doubling)] ISBN: 0-8222-1808-9

★ **PRAYING FOR RAIN by Robert Vaughan.** Examines a burst of fatal violence and its aftermath in a suburban high school. "Thought provoking and compelling." *—Denver Post.* "Vaughan's powerful drama offers hope and possibilities." *—Theatre.com.* "[The play] doesn't put forth compact, tidy answers to the problem of youth violence. What it does offer is a compelling exploration of the forces that influence an individual's choices, and of the proverbial lifelines—be they familial, communal, religious or political—that tragically slacken when society gives in to apathy, fear and self-doubt…" *—Westword.* "…a symphony of anger…" *—Gazette Telegraph.* [4M, 3W] ISBN: 0-8222-1807-0

★ **GOD'S MAN IN TEXAS by David Rambo.** When a young pastor takes over one of the most prestigious Baptist churches from a rip-roaring old preacher-entrepreneur, all hell breaks loose. "…the pick of the litter of all the works at the Humana Festival…" *—Providence Journal.* "…a wealth of both drama and comedy in the struggle for power…" *—LA Times.* "…the first act is so funny…deepens in the second act into a sobering portrait of fear, hope and self-delusion…" *—Columbus Dispatch.* [3M] ISBN: 0-8222-1801-1

★ **JESUS HOPPED THE 'A' TRAIN by Stephen Adly Guirgis.** A probing, intense portrait of lives behind bars at Rikers Island. "…fire-breathing…whenever it appears that JESUS is settling into familiar territory, it slides right beneath expectations into another, fresher direction. It has the courage of its intellectual restlessness…[JESUS HOPPED THE 'A' TRAIN] has been written in flame." *—NY Times.* [4M, 1W] ISBN: 0-8222-1799-6

DRAMATISTS PLAY SERVICE, INC.
440 Park Avenue South, New York, NY 10016 212-683-8960 Fax 212-213-1539
postmaster@dramatists.com www.dramatists.com

NEW PLAYS

★ **THE CIDER HOUSE RULES, PARTS 1 & 2 by Peter Parnell, adapted from the novel by John Irving.** Spanning eight decades of American life, this adaptation from the Irving novel tells the story of Dr. Wilbur Larch, founder of the St. Cloud's, Maine orphanage and hospital, and of the complex father-son relationship he develops with the young orphan Homer Wells. "...luxurious digressions, confident pacing...an enterprise of scope and vigor..." *—NY Times.* "...The fact that I can't wait to see Part 2 only begins to suggest just how good it is..." *—NY Daily News.* "...engrossing...an odyssey that has only one major shortcoming: It comes to an end." *—Seattle Times.* "...outstanding...captures the humor, the humility...of Irving's 588-page novel..." *—Seattle Post-Intelligencer.* [9M, 10W, doubling, flexible casting] PART 1 ISBN: 0-8222-1725-2 PART 2 ISBN: 0-8222-1726-0

★ **TEN UNKNOWNS by Jon Robin Baitz.** An iconoclastic American painter in his seventies has his life turned upside down by an art dealer and his ex-boyfriend. "...breadth and complexity...a sweet and delicate harmony rises from the four cast members...Mr. Baitz is without peer among his contemporaries in creating dialogue that spontaneously conveys a character's social context and moral limitations..." *—NY Times.* "...darkly funny, brilliantly desperate comedy...TEN UNKNOWNS vibrates with vital voices." *—NY Post.* [3M, 1W] ISBN: 0-8222-1826-7

★ **BOOK OF DAYS by Lanford Wilson.** A small-town actress playing St. Joan struggles to expose a murder. "...[Wilson's] best work since *Fifth of July*...An intriguing, prismatic and thoroughly engrossing depiction of contemporary small-town life with a murder mystery at its core...a splendid evening of theater..." *—Variety.* "...fascinating...a densely populated, unpredictable little world." *—St. Louis Post-Dispatch.* [6M, 5W] ISBN: 0-8222-1767-8

★ **THE SYRINGA TREE by Pamela Gien.** Winner of the 2001 Obie Award. A breathtakingly beautiful tale of growing up white in apartheid South Africa. "Instantly engaging, exotic, complex, deeply shocking...a thoroughly persuasive transport to a time and a place...stun[s] with the power of a gut punch..." *—NY Times.* "Astonishing...affecting ...[with] a dramatic and heartbreaking conclusion...A deceptive sweet simplicity haunts THE SYRINGA TREE..." *—A.P.* [1W (or flexible cast)] ISBN: 0-8222-1792-9

★ **COYOTE ON A FENCE by Bruce Graham.** An emotionally riveting look at capital punishment. "The language is as precise as it is profane, provoking both troubling thought and the occasional cheerful laugh...will change you a little before it lets go of you." *—Cincinnati CityBeat.* "...excellent theater in every way..." *—Philadelphia City Paper.* [3M, 1W] ISBN: 0-8222-1738-4

★ **THE PLAY ABOUT THE BABY by Edward Albee.** Concerns a young couple who have just had a baby and the strange turn of events that transpire when they are visited by an older man and woman. "An invaluable self-portrait of sorts from one of the few genuinely great living American dramatists...rockets into that special corner of theater heaven where words shoot off like fireworks into dazzling patterns and hues." *—NY Times.* "An exhilarating, wicked...emotional terrorism." *—NY Newsday.* [2M, 2W] ISBN: 0-8222-1814-3

★ **FORCE CONTINUUM by Kia Corthron.** Tensions among black and white police officers and the neighborhoods they serve form the backdrop of this discomfiting look at life in the inner city. "The creator of this intense...new play is a singular voice among American playwrights...exceptionally eloquent..." *—NY Times.* "...a rich subject and a wise attitude." *—NY Post.* [6M, 2W, 1 boy] ISBN: 0-8222-1817-8

DRAMATISTS PLAY SERVICE, INC.
440 Park Avenue South, New York, NY 10016 212-683-8960 Fax 212-213-1539
postmaster@dramatists.com www.dramatists.com

NEW PLAYS

★ **PROOF by David Auburn.** Winner of the 2001 Pulitzer Prize. The story of a young woman who gave up everything to care for her brilliant father and what it takes to get it back. "When we think of the great American playwrights, we think of Arthur Miller and Eugene O'Neill and Lillian Hellman, in earlier generations; Wendy Wasserstein and Tony Kushner, Jon Robin Baitz and Donald Margulies today...Welcome David Auburn to the club. PROOF is the one you won't want to miss this fall." –*NY Magazine*. "...combines elements of mystery and surprise with old-fashioned stroytelling to provide a compelling evening of theatre...[a] smart and compassionate play of ideas." –*NY Daily News*. [2M, 2W] ISBN: 0-8222-1782-1

★ **THE LARAMIE PROJECT by Moisés Kaufman and the Members of Tectonic Theatre Project.** A breathtaking theatrical collage that explores the 1998 murder of a twenty-one-year-old student, who was kidnapped, severely beaten and left to die, tied to a fence on the outskirts of Laramie, Wyoming. "There emerges a mosaic as moving and important as any you will see on the walls of the churches of the world...nothing short of stunning...you will be held in rapt attention." –*NY Magazine*. "...an amazing piece of theatre...leaves us sadder, wiser and tentatively more hopeful..." –*NY Post*. [4M, 4W (doubling, flexible casting)] ISBN: 0-8222-1780-5

★ **LOBBY HERO by Kenneth Lonergan.** When a luckless young security guard is drawn into a local murder investigation, loyalties are strained to the breaking point. "Soon after making the year's best movie...Kenneth Lonergan delights us with his irrepressible LOBBY HERO, confirming him as a comic wizard." –*NY Magazine*. "A masterpiece. The best drama, the best comedy and the best romance of the year..." –*Time Out*. [3M, 1W] ISBN: 0-8222-1829-1

★ **BAT BOY by Keythe Farley, Brian Flemming and Laurence O'Keefe.** A musical comedy/horror show about a half boy/half bat creature who's discovered in a cave in West Virginia. "Big laughs...It's remarkable what intelligent wit can accomplish—a jaggedly imaginative mix of skewering humor and energetic glee." –*NY Times*. "Outrageously silly and totally charming." –*NY Daily News*. [6M, 4W (doubling, flexible casting)] ISBN: 0-8222-1834-8

★ **DINNER WITH FRIENDS by Donald Margulies.** Winner of the 2000 Pulitzer Prize. A married couple comes apart, causing their best friends to question their own relationship. "...Margulies writes about relationships with such intelligence and spiky humor that his comedy-drama...becomes something quite wonderful." –*Time Magazine*. "...wry and keenly observed and bathed in the unspoken sorrow that can sneak up on you in middle age..." –*NY Times*. [2M, 2W] ISBN: 0-8222-1754-6

★ **THE UNEXPECTED MAN by Yasmina Reza, translated by Christopher Hampton.** Two strangers on a train: one a famous author, the other a great admirer of his—will she have the nerve to bring his latest book out of her bag and read it; or better still, will she have the nerve to speak to him? "Reza's artful play may persuade you that there is nothing of greater value in all the world than a brief encounter between strangers on a train." –*The New Yorker*. [1M, 1W] ISBN: 0-8222-1793-7

★ **FAME TAKES A HOLIDAY by Cassandra Danz, Mary Fulham and Warren Leight.** A hilarious musical about a female sketch-comedy group striving to succeed in show business against the odds...and its own members. "A light-hearted charmer...takes the audience on a funny, sometimes silly ride...[evokes a] happy nostalgia tinged with a slight contemporary edge." –*BackStage*. "...[a] celebration of both girlishness and womanliness and its affection for the female iconography of the mid-twentieth century is difficult to resist...clever lyrics...entertaining, original tunes." –*NY Times*. [4W] ISBN: 0-8222-1796-1

DRAMATISTS PLAY SERVICE, INC.
440 Park Avenue South, New York, NY 10016   212-683-8960   Fax 212-213-1539
postmaster@dramatists.com   www.dramatists.com

DURANG/DURANG
by Christopher Durang

MRS. SORKEN, a middle-aged suburban matron is scheduled to give a lecture on the meaning of theatre, but has lost her notes. Relying on memory, her comments are dotty, but definitely endearing. (1W).

FOR WHOM THE SOUTHERN BELLE TOLLS. In this parody of THE GLASS MENAGERIE, the fading Southern belle, Amanda, tries to prepare her hyper-sensitive, hypochondriacal son, Lawrence, for "the feminine caller." Terrified of people, Lawrence plays with his collection of glass cocktail stirrers. Ginny, the feminine caller, is hard of hearing and overbearingly friendly. Brother Tom wants to go the movies, where he keeps meeting sailors who need to be put up in his room. Amanda tries to face everything with "charm and vivacity," but sometimes she just wants to hit somebody. (2M, 2W).

A STYE OF THE EYE. In this parody of Sam Shepard's A LIE OF THE MIND, cowboy Jake is a rage-oholic who has probably killed his wife, Beth (played by a male). Ma, his feisty, no-nonsense mother with a bad memory, thinks Beth "deserved" it and wishes her own husband were dead (he already is). Jake, also schizoid, becomes his own "good brother Frankie" and goes to find Beth's family. Beth shows up, not dead, but damaged, and talking gibberish. Jake's sister, Mae, also shows up, in love with her brother. No problems are solved, but a great deal of "meaning" is in the air. (3M, 4W).

NINA IN THE MORNING is a style piece à la Edward Gorey. A tuxedoed narrator presents Nina, a preposterously narcissistic wealthy woman, attended by her butler, a silent maid, and her three children. The interwoven time-frame juxtaposes scenes from Nina's past misbehaviors with the present morning when she can't seem to get the butler to bring her a cruller. (3M, 1-2W, flexible casting).

WANDA'S VISIT. Jim and Marsha have been married for 13 years and are feeling a little bored and unhappy. Wanda, Jim's old girlfriend, shows up for a visit, and becomes the guest from hell. Out one night for dinner, all hell breaks loose in the restaurant as a waiter tries to cope on his first day with the confused threesome. (2-3M, 2-3W, flexible casting).

BUSINESS LUNCH AT THE RUSSIAN TEA ROOM. Chris, a writer, has a business meeting at the Russian Tea Room with a new Hollywood hotshot, Melissa. At the Tea Room, Melissa pitches insane ideas to Chris who can't wait to just leave this meeting. Once home, he tries so hard to write up the idea of a priest and a rabbi who fall in love (and other complications), that they appear to him to help him through. (3M, 3W).

"With the help of Mr. Durang, the fine art of parody has returned to theater in a production you can sink teeth and mind into, while also laughing like an idiot. Parody of this comic verve is as much fun as the sort of marvelous party Noel Coward once sang about. I couldn't have enjoyed it more."
— **The New York T**

"If you need a break from serious drama, the place to go is Christopher Durang's silly, funny the-top sketches, DURANG/DURANG."
—**Theater**

Also by Christopher Durang
LAUGHING WILD
THE MARRIAGE OF BETTE AND BOO
BABY WITH THE BATHWATER
THE ACTOR'S NIGHTMARE
and many others

DRAMATISTS PLAY SERVICE, INC.

ISBN 0-8222-1460-1

9 780822 214601